# LILLIAN TOO'S
## 168 Feng Shui Ways to
## Energize your Life

# Lillian Too's
# 168 Feng Shui Ways to
# Energize your Life

**CICO BOOKS**
LONDON  NEW YORK

Published in 2007 by CICO Books
an imprint of Ryland Peters & Small
20–21 Jockey's Fields, London WC1R 4BW

www.cicobooks.co.uk

10 9 8 7 6 5 4 3 2 1

A CIP catalogue record for this book is available from
the British Library

ISBN-13: 978 1 904991 94 6
ISBN-10: 1 904991 94 7

Printed in China

Editor: Robin Gurdon
Designer: Jerry Goldie
Illustrators: Stephen Dew and
Anthony Duke

# Contents

CHAPTER FOUR
## Tapping into Your Inner Spiritual Power

CHAPTER FIVE
## Creating Powerful Personal Charisma

# INTRODUCTION

**E**nergy is our most precious gift from the cosmos. Ever since mankind's existence began in the churning of the great oceans, the spark that gives us life is the energy within us. It is from our own energy source that the essence of our being is derived, enabling us to take pleasure from our relationships – both in giving and in receiving – and is what causes us to benefit from our work and our ambitions. It is the source from which we draw our spiritual strength, improve our physical appearance and actualize all our aims and desires, in the process benefiting both others and ourselves.

It is when we become conscious of our energy, knowing how we can nurture and tap into it, that life becomes meaningful. As we become aware of its great potency we start to feel our invisible auras. Human auras comprise spinning wheels of energy whose radiance directly reflects our inner well-being. They manifest as colours invisible to us but which special cameras have captured. When the aura is weak, the energy level of the person is also weak and when the aura is strong there is simply no mistaking it. That is when the aura glows thick and bright around a person.

## Let your aura vibrate

When the aura around you is robust your home will vibrate with your personal energy. Human abodes resonate in tandem with the humans that live within them, and especially those residents whose auras reflect their vibrant personas. Thus the auras of homes are powerful and strong when residents are energized but are weak when residents are listless and down. If your aura vibrates with happiness and confidence, your homes give out the same energy and this is the source of good luck and good fortune. Good energy homes and people are incredibly potent in manifesting feelings of satisfaction, in fulfilling needs and in actualizing goals. In short, in manifesting happiness.

In recent years, energy has become more understood, people now talk about it like an old friend. There is an enthusiasm to discover how this energy can be tapped, enhanced and strengthened as if the energy surrounding you can be improved you will enhance your personal charisma, increase your effectiveness and be like a magnet to wealth, health, fabulous relationships.

This then is what this book is about: feng shui as a living skill is, above all things, about improving the energy around us. It is about clarifying the energy inside homes and getting rid of stale or imported negatives that cause suffering from bad luck, the unhappy vibrations

Sacred objects in the home help focus good energy.

and, worst of all, the sudden reversals of fortune.

## Understanding energy

Good energy that safeguards and improves luck but it goes beyond living and workspaces. The energy of the individual is equally as important (if not more so).

This book also focuses on how individuals can work on improving their intrinsic inner energy. There are sections dealing with different techniques of raising mental awareness levels and using the mind to create radiant images of success. Other sections direct attention towards tapping into the deeply spiritual aspects of the self, for it is only when we engage our spiritual side that we can delve deeper into our inner more powerful selves.

## Emanate self-belief

We also work with the living tenets that have been advised by ancient masters of healing whose 'thousands of observations' provide the important guidelines we can use to preserve our physical wellbeing and improve our outward appearances. So there is a section devoted to the principles behind not just good looks but powerful good looks. The idea is to enhance our charisma and personal magnetism.

Finally there is a section on how we should school ourselves to become real pros at what we each do. This includes the things we need to do to improve our physical spaces to fire up all aspects of our lives.

When you energize yourself and your space, all dimensions of the self improve. All work done on improving the self has spill-over effects in all areas of your life. The feng shui energizing tips covered here are

Use meditation to discover the power of your aura.

thus incredibly beneficial. Remember that energy is something mankind has had since the beginning of time. The ancients from many cultures knew about energy; only they called it different names and they represented the end result as magic, attributing energy's potency to some supernatural or spiritual outside force.

## Energy's spiritual power

Perhaps energy IS spiritual; maybe our personal energy is not only linked to the energy of our environment and our homes; maybe it is also linked to other dimensions of existence and to other parallel worlds. But whatever these links are, the potency of energy is acknowledged, only the cause and source of it has not been fully explored. Explanations about the potency of energy are incomplete simply because we have yet to discover more about it. We know that when we do certain things our energy gets revitalized but we do not know how this happens. For instance we know that when we have sufficient sleep our energy gets replenished and we are sharper, clearer in our thinking and more radiant in our appearance. Conventional wisdom offers a simple enough explanation – more rest equates to a stronger mind and body hence making our intrinsic energy stronger as well. But there is more to it ...

## The magical breath of cosmic chi

Energy as we now define it – as something deeply potent and powerful within us – has never really been described or explained directly. References to energy were always expressed in symbolic terms. The Chinese collective consciousness has always revolved around symbolism and the easiest way for people to understand energy was to create stories and legends around its seemingly magical powers.

Thus was born the symbolism of the dragon's cosmic chi, the magical breath that energizes, gives vitality, brings luck, builds confidence and manifests as the ten thousand things that create universal happiness. Over time the Chinese began to refer to this life essence as chi, developing the exercises known as chi kung and feng shui, the art of harnessing the dragon's chi. There is also traditional Chinese medicine, which diagnoses ailments and offers cures according to the conditions of yin and yang chi within the human body.

## The power of charisma

There are people whose energy is so powerful that all who meet and interact with them feel their energy. People like this radiate an almost irresistible charisma, an energy that is unseen but most definitely felt. Such people are described as compelling, alluring, and captivating – there is no shortage of adjectives.

The source of their magnetism comes from an inner fire that glows from within. Such powerful people are always blessed with a full audience. Their words possess a force that is inspiring to experience.

What is the source of such people's energy?

Where does their radiance come from?

This book will help you gain some of these energy levels. Gone forever will be the effects of overwork, stress, exhaustion, indecisiveness and lack of focus that reflect energy at a low ebb.

## The dangers of yin spirits

If you allow negative attitudes to keep piling up there is no way good chi will come to you. Over the days, weeks or even months, your home will reflect your inner listlessness, with clutter accumulating and dust gathering under furniture and cupboards. In your gardens weeds grow and good plants die through lack of care. In feng shui we describe this condition as yin spirit formation.

## The solution is to re-energize

It is this that will help you to create pathways to success and to energize your life forever. Many are age-old secrets that work for everyone. Some of the tips you pick up from this book may be things you already knew, or you may have already been unconsciously doing. That should not surprise you. These 'secrets' are sometimes already known to us, stored in our subconscious from past lives or lying dormant, forgotten by our conscious mind. Often we do things that are good for us without us even realizing.

The best way to use re-energizing techniques and to make sure they work really well is to develop the ability to concentrate, to tightly focus attention each time you do any of the mental exercises I recommend. Remember this above all as you work your way through the 168 techniques summarized in this book!

# Chapter One

# Getting to Grips With Energy-Stealers

How can harnessing our own intrinsic energy work? How does activating the energy of our space make a difference to our lives? The key to our vigour and our strength, our success and our happiness lies in the quality of our internal and external energy. This is why energy is such a vital part of our being.

If you want to learn about revitalizing energy, the best place to begin is familiar territory. Start with a room in which you spend a considerable amount of time, and which you have occupied for at least six months. This is the best place to work at developing awareness of space and energy.

If you have never put undivided attention into the energy of your room before, begin by consciously tuning into its energy. Here's how.

# 1  Attune your senses

Stand in the centre of your room and direct your attention to its corners, pivoting in a clockwise direction and taking note of all the furniture and decorative objects... in fact, everything around you. Let your eyes send their messages to your mind when you tune into the room's energy. You need your five senses to work in cooperation with each other so you can also become aware of sounds – of water dripping, the breeze murmuring through the window and even the radio playing – and activate touch sensations with the palms of your hands.

Go slow to become aware of the energy of your room. Note your observations, but the idea is to train your mind to tune into your living space. Be as meticulous as possible in the way you take note of the many things inside your room. Every little thing has energy and all energy is different, possessing different wavelengths and different affinities.

Turn your thoughts to the spaces and the objects of the room. Become aware of physical structures that make up the room, the height and colour of walls, the occurrence of beams, doors and windows, exposed pipes and protrusions. Try not to miss anything. Direct your mind to make mental notes of the room's arrangement and decorations.

**Feel it!**

Next, tune into the feel of the room. Does it feel tired? Is the energy stagnant? Does the thought of giving it a makeover enter your mind at all? Is the room too dark? Should you be installing more lights? Are the curtains in need of a wash? Is the carpet feeling a bit damp? Are the light bulbs working? Does sunlight enter the room at all?

These and a thousand questions should come unprompted as you assess the space you are familiar with. In no time at all your comfort with the familiar surroundings will help you to communicate with the spirit energy of your room. When the room begins exchanging thoughts with you it will direct your attention to the things you need to be aware of.

If you use the room exclusively, the 'you' energy of the room will be dominant. If the room feels happy you can be certain you are both the cause and beneficiary of the happy energy. If the room feels stagnant, you are also its cause and its result. The energy of the room mirrors your state of mind, so when you change the energy of your living space you will immediately change your life. Stimulate it with fresh new energy and you will feel revitalized and recharged.

When you tune into your senses, you tap into the unique energy of the spaces in your home.

# Mentally take orientations 2

Your ability to tune into the energy of a room becomes a lot more powerful when you actively engage the tools of feng shui. Let your mental awareness take on improved clarity by adding technical correctness to your observations. Everything placed in the eight different corners of a room has an effect on its feng shui, some more significantly so than others. Each corner signifies a compass direction, and you will discover that every corner has a different feng shui attribute. For now, simply register an awareness of the items in the different corners of your room.

## Start with a compass

Get yourself a good compass and use it to take the orientations of the room. Fix the compass points firmly in your mind. If you need to, have a floor plan of your room to hand to mark out compass locations. It is a good idea to commit the compass orientations of your room to memory. Let this vital information seep into your inner consciousness, especially if you plan to continue occupying the room. Becoming firmly aware of the orientation of your living arrangements will help you anchor the feng shui interpretations associated with the different corners of your room.

## What to do

Stand in the centre of your room and mentally mark out different corners. Take note of where the door into the room is located, which compass corner it is in and what direction it faces. Get used to thinking in terms of compass directions and sectors.

Open the door and look at what lies outside. Is there a staircase directly facing the door? If so

that could be bad, and you might want to make a mental note to always keep the door closed or immediately place some kind of curtain to soften the energy directly coming from the staircase. There are other afflictive things you need to look out for, which we will come to later (see Tips 44–68).

## Bedrooms, bathrooms

Let your gaze move round each room in the same way, registering the location of the toilet, bed, cupboards and so forth. Every piece of furniture has an effect on the chi of the room, and will affect your wellbeing.

The Lo Pan compass reveals all the element and other feng shui attributes of the different compass directions.

### ENERGY TIP

## Using a room plan

Your compass and room plan are vital feng shui tools. To help assess your space, sketch out a room using graph paper, adding all the key items of furniture, fixtures and fittings, before allocating the eight compass directions.

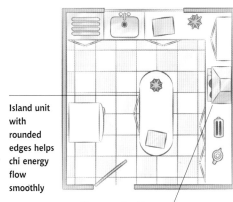

Island unit with rounded edges helps chi energy flow smoothly

The stove should never be next to the sink

Include smaller items such as plants and ornaments in your room plan, because these contribute to the balance of elements in a room.

# 3 Spotting energy-stealers around you

It is easy to miss the things that bring you harm in your environment unless you concentrate on registering everything that has a place in your space.

This is why you need to engage your mind one hundred percent and why it is necessary to develop a keen awareness when you look around your room, otherwise you can miss things that you would normally take for granted. Those new to feng shui almost always have preconceived ideas about what is, or is not, important from a feng shui perspective. The truth of the matter, of course, is that everything can be important. That is why it is helpful to develop an awareness of energy. This is the key to determining its impact on your feng shui.

The overhead beam creates poison arrows

Seating placed directly below the beam is afflicted

## Watch out for the little things

An awareness of energy leads to direct communication with the spirit of a room. This helps to draw your attention to features that have a negative effect upon you; for instance, newspapers piled up in a corner that corresponds to your success direction create obstacles to your success. In the hall, shoes caked with mud left near your front door will cause negative energy to be sent to the door, while a dirty ashtray placed in the middle of the living room or wall paint that is peeling in the northwest corner will affect the man of the family. A chip on a coffee cup usually brings hiccups to well-laid plans; the sharp edge of a sideboard hitting you as you sleep will affect your chances

Shoes lined up by the door can create negative, blocked energy, stopping good fortune entering the home.

of success at work, and the heavy energy of a beam directly above your bed can be the cause of migraines and tension. These are things that can easily escape a busy person's attention.

If you are a career person who comes home tired each day you may not have the time or inclination to notice your surroundings, let alone become aware of things that could be hurting you, so do not be surprised if you are totally oblivious to the way energy is moving (or not moving) in your rooms. By the time you wake up to the fact that a host of energy-stealers have been pressing down on your energy, you might well be too weak to do anything – so now is the time to turn energy-detective.

# Developing the all-seeing feng shui eye    4

The more clued in you are to your living space, the more observant you will become in terms of identifying the source of good and bad energy. You need to practice developing an all-seeing feng shui eye.

## Zone in!

Observe the shape of the room, its height, size and most importantly the orientation of sitting and/or sleeping directions based on the arrangement of the furniture. Take note of each item's shape, colour, size and placement, and see how they interact. Observe also the decorative objects, computers, and other things placed on tables, in cupboards and in the corners. These things make up the sum total of the energy of any room. So look at everything that adds to the ambience.

Whatever the decorative style of your rooms, don't let familiar possessions become invisible. Every item impacts upon the feng shui of the room, and therefore its intrinsic energy.

**Check out the art on your wall – is it positive and uplifting?**

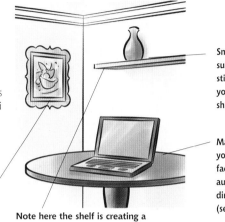

**Small items such as vases still affect your feng shui**

**Make sure you sit facing your auspicious direction (see Tip 68)**

**Note here the shelf is creating a poison arrow hitting the person sat at the computer**

The all-seeing feng shui eye is like a camera in your mind. Click a picture making sure that you are using a wide-angle lens, then focus on it until you remember it easily. This is a crucial part of the inner feng shui method that requires you to use your mental concentration. With a detailed and clear mental image, your efforts at creating new energy or strengthening existing energy will be much more effective.

Awareness levels always improve with practice – soon you will be able to bring an image to mind at a click of your fingers!

Use your feng shui eye to absorb every item in a room and recall the image at will.

15

# 5    Mental sun-ray cleansing

One of the most beneficial things that you can do each morning as soon as you open your eyes from sleep is to think happy thoughts. Focus on generating a feeling of great happiness to be alive, awake and well. This creates good energy that you can harness to mentally cleanse your bedroom with 'morning energy'.

## Creating the right images

It seems very simple to wake up to thoughts of happiness at just being alive, but this is a very powerful and very purifying thought-ritual. Many Asian cultures incorporate this waking-up yoga into their morning rituals, although it is known only to practitioners of meditative skills. Old Taoist masters of the esoteric sciences are well versed with these and other meditative imaging, and they do it as a matter of habit when waking up every day.

---

**ENERGY TIP**

## Take a light bath at work

This is a five-minute daily exercise that is extremely beneficial as it creates a good base of yang energy at work. This strengthens whatever else you may do to re-energize your work space but, more importantly, the happy energy you will emanate will boost all your work relationships, along with your confidence.

1 Sit quietly at your desk, and relax by taking a deep, slow breath. Imagine that you are waking up in your bed, bathed in pure sunshine energy.

2 Visualize yellow light radiating outwards, becoming white and then merging with the space.

---

## Radiate the sunshine aura

Radiating the sunshine aura means radiating feelings of wellbeing from the moment you wake up. Inspired by the rays of the sun. it's a meditation technique that is so easy to master.

## How to do it

When you come out of sleep mode and become fully conscious of your surroundings, visualize a bright yellow light above the crown of your head slowly expanding and radiating outwards – this is the sun lighting up your surroundings. Feel the gentle warmth of the imagined sun as it radiates rays of heat and light outwards. These yellow rays transform into white and soon dissolve into the space around you, transforming the energy of your space, ridding it of the yin influences of the night and infusing it instead with the morning's yang energy.

# Be alert to negativity! 6

It is always important to stay alert to negative feelings. These are the outward manifestations of intuitively felt negative energy impacting upon our consciousness. Not many people realize that negative feelings, responses and emotions, which are usually encountered as negative news, metamorphose into negative outcomes – each a direct result of some hostile energy caused by bad influences.

## Where hostility comes from

The source of bad influences can be other people's energy so we react to them with anger, envy, jealousy, impatience and a host of other similar negative feelings. If we absorb other people's bad energy it can affect the weak amongst us.

Bad influences càn also be picked up from any of the powerful and potentially harmful sources of energy in the external environment, sending sharp doses of invisible poison at us that affect our energy without us realizing it. This bad energy is like poison and it brings misfortune, bad luck, sudden reversals of fortune, accidents, disease and ill health. Everything that makes life unpleasant is brought about by poisonous energy, which can cause stagnation, create a heavy depressive feeling or, worst of all, can also bring a killing result, something that results in total loss of everything. Yes, debilitating and malicious energy can be this overpowering.

## Countering bad energy

This is why it is so important to be alert to bad energy. The most simple examples can be found in everyday concerns we are all aware of – polluted air versus clean air; breathtaking scenery versus smoky skylines; clean lakes versus dirty drains. It is so much more auspicious to live in a beautiful, residential neighbourhood than in or near overcrowded high-rise dwellings. If you can, always choose to live in neighbourhoods that feel happy, clean and auspicious.

If you want a meaningful and happy life, start by choosing an external environment that will help you grow, bring you luck and energize you on a daily basis.

Using feng shui to protect you from negativity is like using an umbrella to shield you from life's storms.

# 7    Neutralize hurtful buildings

Although most of us are stuck in our present location and it is usually quite hard to counter bad energy in the external environment, it is better, nevertheless, to be aware of anything that may be creating problems for your home in terms of surrounding energy. Once you develop your powers of observation, turn your attention to the environment around you, looking for both natural and man-made features outside.

What hurt most are tall and hostile looking buildings that directly face your house. Large structures that stand right in front of your house usually cause obstacles in your life, creating blocking energies that bring misfortune and cause you to fail.

## Size and shape matter

Some buildings are more harmful than others. Those with many corners and edges are the source of the greatest amounts of negative energy. When buildings are tilted, thereby causing their edges to point directly at your home, it is very dangerous. The edge of a building is like a knife-edge that sends very sharp killing energy your way.

The colour of tiles and walls of buildings, as well as the shape of the building itself, can be a severe problem especially if the colours and shapes represent elements unfriendly to the element of your home.

## Which destructive energy could affect your home?

- A home that sits **south** (facing north) is a fire-element house, so if the building opposite you is a curvilinear shape and is predominantly blue or black, signifying water, the energy being sent your way represents killing energy. It must be neutralized with earth element energy. Solve this problem by building a brick wall.

- If your home sits **north** (facing south) it is said to be a water-element house. If the building opposite is round and predominantly yellow, signifying earth, the energy being sent your way represents destructive energy – it must be neutralized with wood-element energy. Planting a tree or growing a hedge will combat this.

- A home that sits **east** (facing west) or southeast (ie facing northwest) is a wood-element house, so if the building opposite is square and predominantly white or metallic, thereby signifying metal, the energy being sent your way represents destructive energy, which must be neutralized with fire-element energy – try installing bright lights.

- When your home sits **west** (facing east) or **northwest** (facing southeast), it is a metal-element house. A triangular shape and predominantly red, signifying fire, the energy being sent your way, represents destructive energy – neutralize it with water-element energy by building a small fountain.

- If your home sits **northeast** (facing southwest) or **southwest** (facing northeast), it is an earth-element house, and if the building opposite is rectangular and mostly brown or green, signifying wood, the energy coming your way represents destructive energy. Neutralize it with metal-element energy; using a windchime will help.

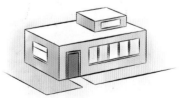

# Beware the straight road at a T-junction 8

The number of roads that directly face your house can have a serious impact on its feng shui. Generally speaking, the T-junction is one of the deadliest since this means the house or building directly faces a long, straight road. When the traffic is moving fast towards the house or building the feng shui is extraordinarily bad as it hits the building with killing energy, called shar chi; and when the traffic is flowing away from the building it is taking away all the wealth of the building with it. So either way a straight road in front of your house, or even in front of your apartment building, brings bad luck. Thus the T-junction is super bad news whichever way the road moves.

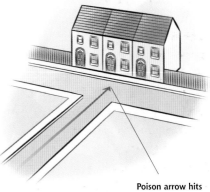

The T-junction road creates a poison arrow aimed at the house door aligned with the centre of the T shape.

**Poison arrow hits the front door here**

T-junction properties can be less afflicted by poison arrows if they are raised above the level of the road.

## Poison arrows

Poison arrows are an example of seriously afflicted energy in your external environment. Remember, anything straight that is aimed directly at your house, and especially your front door, is like having killing energy 'shooting' the residents.

When there are two buildings with a narrow road separating them directly in front of your house, the effect is considered severe. The road's energy is similar to that of the straight road possessing the energy of a harmful poison arrow aimed at your house. This effect can cause accidents and misfortune.

People living in houses hit by such unfriendly energy are sure to experience difficulties manifesting in different areas of their life, and many of these difficulties cause distress and have tragic consequences. The Chinese have always avoided straight roads pointed directly at their homes or their offices. If your home is elevated above the level of the road however the T-junction road is not so harmful, otherwise it is considered a cardinal source of negative energy.

# 9 Getting hit by multi-level roads

Another kind of road that is a part of modern cityscapes is the multi-level highway, which can bring thundering traffic precariously close to homes, especially the small apartments that are often sited inside high-rise buildings.

When these elevated roads 'embrace' your home they are not so harmful, but if your apartment is located at the outside bend of the road they are said to be cutting into your home. There is little that can be done if you are being 'hit' by elevated roads apart from using heavy curtains to block them from view.

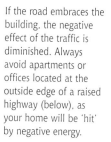

If the road embraces the building, the negative effect of the traffic is diminished. Always avoid apartments or offices located at the outside edge of a raised highway (below), as your home will be 'hit' by negative energy.

# 10 Being sandwiched between two roads

When your home is located between two busy roads, the energy they generate can be very harmful. Both the front and back of the house are vulnerable to harmful environmental energy, described in feng shui terminology as 'being squeezed between two tigers' – and this suggests something very unpleasant happening to residents.

The situation is made worse if one of the roads is higher than the other, and even more so when the higher road is at the front of the house. This strongly tilts the home's energy completely out of balance, bringing unstable luck to residents. In such a case, no matter how excellent the energy of your personal living space is, it becomes really hard to enjoy good fortune.

**Overcoming the two tigers**

When two roads hug the back and front of your home, build a high wall at the back to create a barrier between your property and the road. If the two roads are sandwiching the two sides of the dwelling the effect is not so bad, especially if the building is big in relation to the roads.

This countryside dwelling has poor feng shui as it is trapped between two busy roads, creating an overload of yang energy.

# Fast-moving highways create killer energies    11

Surrounding roads can be a source of furious and fast-moving energy, and if you live near such highways they can cause you a great deal of problems as the excessive yang energy created must be tempered. The best way to deal with this problem is to build a wall-like barrier that effectively shuts out the negative noise and energy of the highway.

The key to assessing if roads can send damaging energy towards you is the distance between your house and the road – the nearer you are, the more you will feel the bullet energy of cars speeding by.

But usually, as long as you are able to create some kind of barrier – trees, wall, a hedge – it will make a world of difference. In feng shui what you do not see visually is deemed to have been effectively blocked, as any energy created cannot reach you.

Shrubs and trees can screen your home from traffic if you live on a busy road.

# Does your home face a circular interchange?    12

When your home faces a circular interchange such as a roundabout, the effect of the circular energy on your home depends on how fast the traffic is flowing and whether the roads seem to bring a flow of chi energy to your home. Thus fast-flowing traffic is bad while slow-moving traffic is good. When the traffic seems to flow naturally towards your home without appearing to be hostile, the circular road brings good energy and thus good fortune, but if it seems to be flowing away from your home it is considered to be taking wealth away from the building.

Another approach is element analysis. The circular nature of the road interchange makes it a metal-element situation and for homes that 'sit' in a north direction (which means they are facing south) the metal energy of the interchange brings good fortune.

Modern houses tend to have circular interchanges or turning areas

Flow of yang energy

Fast-moving traffic on a circular interchange creates bad energy for your home, draining you of income.

# 13   The effect of feeder roads

When you look at the roads that flow past your home, first note if the road is beneficial or harmful. The effect is said to be beneficial when traffic on the road is moving slowly and gently curving towards your home. This effect is increased if there are feeder roads joining the road before it moves past your main entrance as it is bringing more than one source of wealth to your building. Feeder roads are thus good news in this context.

However, if the road passing your home is fast-moving and harmful then the feeder roads are said to be adding negative energy to the road, and the harmful effect is then increased.

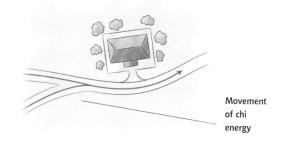

Movement of chi energy

Feeder roads, such as small sliproads with little traffic, are not harmful to the feng shui of your home.

# 14   Becoming aware of harmful man-made structures

Structures such as transmission towers, large factory chimneys or telecommunication towers are infamous for the massive doses of shar chi they send out, and this 'killing breath' is often hard to combat. They may cause illness to those living in houses or apartments nearby. Electricity transmission towers may be especially harmful, and it is advisable to avoid living too close to these buildings.

Other potentially harmful structures that can cause feng shui problems for you if you live too near them are big steel and chrome bridges, power stations and other massive concrete and steel edifices.

Be extremely wary of man-made constructions. They are not only threatening; they are also often the source of killing energy, especially when they face your home directly. Put some visual distance between you and such structures by planting some trees to create a barrier of leaves between them and your home.

Take a look over the terrace or balcony – you may have high walls or fencing around you, but external structures can still influence the feng shui of your property.

Triangular-shaped roofs can create poison arrows

Bamboo screening can help shield some negativity from neighbours' buildings

# Effective cures against harm-bringing external structures

# 15

When you have a large hostile building, road or structure, which you suspect is hurting your home, you can select from amongst these five cures based on the direction the harmful energy is coming from as it points towards your house. These methods are based on the compass formulas.

- Hang a **curved knife** outside your house directly confronting the structure if its harmful energy is coming at the house from the east or southeast.

- Place a **large boulder** between your door and the harmful structure if it is coming from the north direction.

- Place a **bright spotlight** above your door so it shines outwards if the hostile building, road or structure is coming from the west or northwest direction.

- Place an **urn of water** in front of your house if the offending structure is coming at you from the south.

- Plant **a clump of trees** in front of the house if the offending structure comes at you from the southwest or northeast.

Place bright lighting outside your home to curb hostile energy coming from the west and northwest directions.

An urn of still water calms negative energy coming from any structures located in the south. This urn also features Kuan Yin, the Buddhist goddess of compassion.

Natural elements such as trees and stone protect your home from negative external structures.

# 16 Coping with unfriendly neighbours

A common problem for many who live in suburbia is the bad vibes that are caused by neighbours, especially those with noisy, naughty children. Neighbours can be very quarrelsome or even hostile and, in the worst cases, downright harmful.

In such cases what can you do? Problems with neighbours are especially trying when you live in terraced houses or in apartment blocks with thin walls. Then the wailing of children and noise can be so trying as to unsettle you hugely. And when they resort to using feng shui against you – they may hang Pa Kua mirrors above their doors that are aimed directly at you – it can even cause you to experience bad luck.

Calm noisy neighbours with a simple bowl of still water – with flowers and candles, it makes a pretty table centrepiece when you want to enjoy a quiet dinner with friends.

## Making a yin water bowl

Take a clean bowl and fill with cold water.

Add a tea light to the centre of the bowl

## Calming the neighbours

One of the most effective cures to calm down noisy and quarrelsome vibes from the residence next to you, opposite you or behind you is to place water in an urn with a large surface area. The water should ideally be still rather than bubbling. We call this yin water.

Then place a light in the centre of the water. This creates a 'dot' of yang energy that makes your yin water more powerful. Place this water (with light feature) near the wall that you share with the neighbour; it will absorb whatever hostile vibes may be coming through the walls before they can hurt you.

This same cure can be used to absorb bad chi caused by Pa Kua mirrors hung across the road, or above the door of the neighbour opposite. Let your water feature 'receive' the bad chi and then transform it into good chi.

# Dissolving bad energy from physical structures   17

Practical feng shui takes account of everything in the physical environment around us that does us harm. What we need to develop is sensitivity to the structures that emit invisible killing energy that is inadvertently directed towards the house, often without us realizing it. It is only when we make a conscious effort to look out for these structures that we notice them.

Harmful energy can come in any form, but mostly it is created by sharp, straight or pointed structures, so straight roads, T-junctions and large buildings that appear intimidating directly in front of the house are what we need to be careful of. In fact, anything that seems threatening and hostile – even an art object with pointed and sharp edges – can be regarded as harmful. In addition, look out for triangular roof lines and the corners of other buildings. These are some of

the more common architectural features that can pose a feng shui problem.

## Countering afflictions

Basic feng shui cures can dissolve these harmful energy-killers. How effective the remedy is depends on the strength of the killing energy coming at the house. Thus large buildings are far more potent as carriers of killing chi than a small telephone box or a light pole. Massive triangular roofs are also more deadly than small ones.

Whatever their strength, however, if you place the correct element cure between your home and the source of killing energy, you can successfully dissolve the bad energy before it hits your house. Usually, cures are recommended based on the destructive cycle of the five elements, which effectively suppress negative energy in the environment (see Tip 18).

Powerful city landscapes can be the cause of negative 'killing' energy due to the concentration of sharp, angular structures.

# 18 Determine the killing element correctly

Here's how to diagnose the element of killing energy so that you can counter its effects with a cure. There are only five elements, but choosing the right one is crucial for the cure to work. You need to be familiar with the killing cycle of the elements:

- Wood kills earth

- Earth kills water

- Water kills fire

- Fire kills metal

- Metal kills wood

Use a compass to determine the source direction of killing energy that is directly hitting your home, and especially your main front door. Every direction is associated with an element. Once you have established the element of killing energy, you can determine the element that will deflect its harmful effects and act as a cure.

## The deflecting element cycle

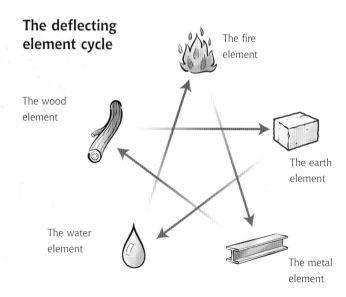

The fire element

The wood element

The earth element

The water element

The metal element

## ENERGY TIP

### Check your directions

Metal energy deflects negative wood energy hitting the home.

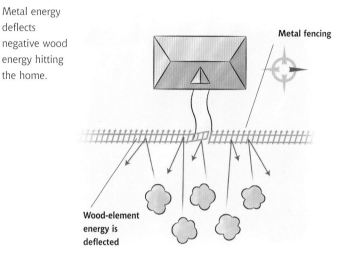

Metal fencing

Wood-element energy is deflected

## The elements associated with directions are as follows:

|  | | |
|---|---|---|
| South | Fire | Water |
| North | Water | Earth |
| East & southeast | Wood | Metal |
| West & northwest | Metal | Fire |
| Southwest & northeast | Earth | Wood |

Use the chart above to discover which element is potentially harmful and its relevant cure. Some examples are:

- When the source of killing energy is south use a fountain of water to deflect fire
- When the source of killing energy is north use a concrete wall to signify earth to soak away water
- When the source of killing energy is east or southeast, use metal railings to enclose the wood
- When the source of killing energy is west or northwest, use bright lights to melt away metal
- When the source of killing energy is southwest or northeast, use a hedge to signify wood to cover the earth

# Overhead beams weigh down on you   21

One of the most harmful of structures in most homes is the exposed overhead beam. Many apartments in older buildings have these harmful beams that send down killing energy to those sitting directly under them. It is worse when the apartment is on the lower floors of a high-rise building, as these structural beams are usually repeated on every floor.

## Blocking bad energy

In bungalows and houses these beams are not as powerful and so are less harmful. To block the bad energy so they do not hurt any member of the household all you have to do is block these beams from views with a carefully designed ceiling... it is also good to arrange your furniture so that your favourite chair is not placed directly under these beams. In homes that have many exposed rafters and raw pieces of wood that

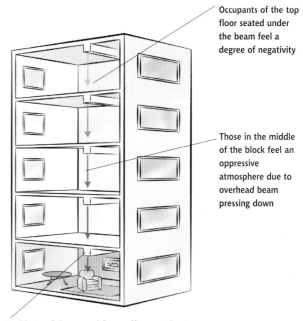

Occupants of the top floor seated under the beam feel a degree of negativity

Those in the middle of the block feel an oppressive atmosphere due to overhead beam pressing down

Residents of the ground floor suffer most due to accumulated effect of the beam over four levels

appear part of the overall design or look of the home, the exposed beams or wood do not create harmful energy. It is only when the overhead beam sticks out like a sore thumb that they can be potentially harmful.

An excellent cure is to install lighting that is directed upwards towards the ceiling, as this has the effect of pushing the energy upwards. It also creates a very soft, subdued effect, softening the energy of a room considerably.

When in doubt, always move your seat if it is situated directly under a beam. Even when you are just visiting a friend, it is a good idea to avoid taking the seat directly under an overhead beam.

## ENERGY TIP
### Using bright lighting

In feng shui, lighting is an excellent cure for oppressive structures overhead.

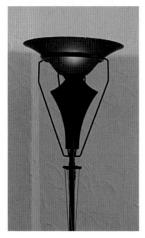

Uplighters can help remedy the negative chi created by overhead beams in your home or office.

# 22 Protruding corners send out killing chi

Sharp edges of walls and furniture are another source of bad energy. The remedy for this inside homes and offices is to place something directly in front of the protruding edge so that they are blocked from view. Camouflaged from view the edges lose their unfriendliness and are transformed from being sources of bad energy into harmless structures that become part of the ambience of a room.

Edges can also be made blunt so the sharpness of the edge disappears thereby losing their threatening energy. Stand-alone square pillars or exposed corners that are the source of misfortune energy can be made harmless this way. If you are on the receiving end of these edges you will tend to be more susceptible to illnesses and accidents. Blunt these edges by literally slicing off the sharp corner or, if they are pillars, wrap them with mirrors. This has the effect of making

Square glass tables such as these look so elegant, but create poison arrows due to multiple sharp corners.

## Positioning mirrors on pillars

Placing a mirror on square pillars as shown above helps to dilute poison arrows that can emanate from each sharp corner of the pillar, creating negative chi in the room.

the pillar merge with the rest of the room, thereby visually blunting the edges.

If you have already used these remedies, remember that these cures need to be renewed. Whatever is placed in front of sharp corners needs to be changed and renewed regularly. Over time remedies lose their strength and must be revitalized. I usually change my cures every New Year (in January or early February, the lunar New Year) to ensure adequate strength to overcome hostile killing energy.

Pieces of furniture such as desks and sideboards also have edges that can create bad energy. In such instances, the solution is to rearrange the desk or cupboard so the edges do not cause a feng shui problem. When you rearrange your rooms, you are in effect moving the energy.

# Staircases that block success    23

The location of internal staircases can have a positive or negative impact on the energy of homes as they serve as conduits of chi, transferring the energy from one level to another. The conduit of energy must be positive and auspicious for good energy to prevail through all the levels of the home.

The best staircases are wide and curving. When gently curved, they encourage the flow of benevolent energy from one level of the house to the next. As straight staircases tend to take on the character of straight poison arrows it is always better to curve the staircase if possible. To energize straight staircases it is a good idea to keep them brightly lit and to hang happy pictures that have the effect of slowing down the energy, thereby transforming any tense energy into benevolent energy.

## Solutions for staircases

If yours is a narrow staircase you should definitely keep it well lit. Make sure that the steps have backs, and are not open; also, avoid steps with decorative holes as these weaken the energy, allowing it to seep away instead of moving up to the next level where it should be strengthened.

Metal staircases are best in the west and northwest, although concrete staircases are also good. Wooden staircases are best in the east and southeast as well as in the south. The idea is to select according to the element of the corner where the staircase is located. Staircases should not be in the centre of the house – they are better by the side of the building.

## Tips and remedies

Staircases should not start or end directly facing the following features or rooms:

A generous, sweeping staircase creates excellent feng shui in the home.

- A door
- A toilet
- A mirror
- The bedroom

as these are blocks to success. Of these taboos, the most harmful is when the staircase begins directly opposite the front door. Remedy this affliction by placing a bright light between the stairs and the door. Better still, block the door with a screen, forcing the chi that enters the house to meander before passing up the stairs.

# 24   Afflicted main doors let in negative energy

An uncluttered outside space leading through the main door to a bright hallway allows cosmic energy into your home.

Poison arrows from the outside environment should never be allowed to hit your main door. They send killing energy which, in hitting the door, infiltrates the home. Make sure that your main door does not face a straight road that leads directly towards it. Similarly the triangular pointed shape of a neighbour's house roof should not hit the main door. Roads and rooflines often cause the most harm in relation to main doors so do watch out for them. These structures block the success of the occupants of the home.

It's best if main doors open out to a clear space. This is the 'bright hall' effect and is most auspicious. Houses whose main door opens out onto playing fields or empty land usually benefit enormously. Cosmic energy is able to settle in front of the house before entering it, bringing fresh vibrant energy into the home.

### Position of the door

Main doors should never face higher land. When the contours of the land slope downward so that

the back of the house is lower than the front, the situation is inauspicious, bringing afflictive energy that blocks success. In such a situation, you should either change the placement of the main door, or if this is not possible, hang a fairly sizeable mirror to reflect the mountain in front.

The main door should never be located directly under a toilet that is located on the floor above. This is a very inauspicious situation and residents living inside such a home may suffer from ill health. They may also find it difficult to achieve prosperity or success. One way of dealing with this problem is to have a bright light shine upwards but this, at best, should be only a temporary solution.

## Hanging a mirror to reflect high ground

This room plan shows where to hang a mirror to reflect a 'mountain' of high ground in front of the main door.

A large mirror hung on the back wall of the living room reflects the 'mountain' seen through the window at the front.

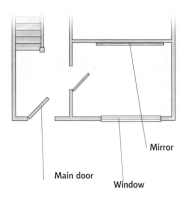

Mirror

Main door   Window

# Blocks outside the door hinder your success    25

Make sure that the energy flowing into your home is never blocked. Physical blockages easily translate into obstacles that prevent you from enjoying success in any of your endeavours. Furniture placed outside the door on verandahs and patios should not encroach on the main door

### A winding path to the door

Any lane or path leading to your main door should be curved and preferably winding. A straight path that leads directly into the home sends in slivers of killing energy. The width of the path should stay constant, neither narrowing towards the house nor away from it. Placing lights on the pathway is auspicious.

A winding path to the main door dispels killing energy along the way. To further enhance positive energy flow, place lit tealights along the edges of the path.

# Allowing only good energy into your home    26

Keep the main door of your home in good condition. If hinges come loose have them repaired immediately. Such damage brings harmful energy into the home and, along with cracks on wooden doors or broken glass panes, signifies loss in your life.

### Letting in fresh cosmic energy

The main door must not face a wall with a mirror on it, as this reflects away good fortune. Fresh cosmic energy cannot enter the home when it is confronted with a mirror, meaning that energy inside the home never gets revitalized. This is often a cause of illness and depression for residents. The main door should not open into a toilet or a staircase, or in a straight line with other doors inside the house. These features transform good energy instantly into harmful energy.

Ideally, the main door to your home will open onto a clear, light hall, and doors to other rooms will not face the main door directly.

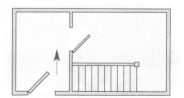

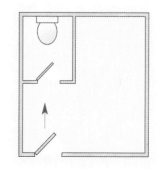

If the main door is opposite a door to a toilet then any fresh, positive energy that comes into your home will be converted into toxic energy.

# 27 Invite yang energy into your home and avoid too much yin energy

*Allowing daylight and fresh air into your home fills it with revitalizing yang energy.*

For the main door to be auspicious, the areas inside and outside it must be well lit. All homes require a continuous topping up of fresh energy from the Cosmos, and the focus of feng shui practice is directed at channelling cosmic energy into your home. Good lighting in the foyer area in the vicinity of the main door attracts cosmic energy.

## Opening doors and windows

Cosmic energy is either yin or yang, and it is daytime cosmic yang energy that brings the benefits we want for a good life, rather than nighttime cosmic yin energy.

One of the best ways of ensuring a good supply of yang chi in all the rooms of your home is to keep doors and windows open through the day. There should be at least one major conduit of flow for yang energy to enter into the home. When the sun sets it is a good idea to close most

of the doors, though keeping the windows open for a while does no harm as a little yin energy balances the yang energy brought in during the day. Always make sure that the energy of the home never gets too yin.

Those who enjoy exercise such as yoga and aerobics, which involve deep breathing, will gain much more benefit during daylight hours. It is more revitalizing to breathe in yang energy than yin energy. If you are unwell, it is especially important to observe this simple rule.

## ENERGY TIP

### Breathing in yang energy

Yoga combines physical postures with deep breaths in and out through the nose to flood the blood around the body with oxygen, revitalizing internal organs. The best time to practise yoga is in the daytime – early morning is ideal – when you will breathe in yang energy. Restorative yoga practice may involve breathing exercises carried out sitting in a simple cross-legged pose.

# Hostile images bring misfortune energy  28

Having sad or hostile images hanging on the walls of your home or office can bring misfortune. The list of potentially harmful images is long. It includes those featuring ferocious animals, grief, dour faces or grim looking portraits. These emanate hostile chi very quickly. Old and grimy images also deaden energy, as do those that have been hanging in unhappy homes.

### Choosing images for positive chi

To determine which images bring negative energy and which do not, trust your first impressions. Consider, for example, whether you find that an image's tones – grades of light and dark – and colours boost your mood or dampen it. Even images of auspicious objects can be harmful when drawn in an inauspicious way.

If you are a lover of art, be careful what you collect and what you hang inside your home. Although art is a matter of individual preference, taking a feng shui perspective can save you from introducing bad energy into your home or office, and lead you instead to choose images that emanate positive chi.

A cluster of mainly dark images creates negative chi in a room that might otherwise be invigorated by the yang energy of the mandarin-coloured sofa.

A large picture of a serene landscape with a river and broad expanse of sky emanates tranquillity and positive chi. The effect is enhanced by hanging the picture on an otherwise uncluttered wall.

# 29 Beware pictures of scary people

A dark image from a gothic horror movie has its own negative energy.

When hanging portraits – or other figure images – in your home, be especially aware of the associations they have for you. Ancestors, as well as prints or paintings of artists, celebrities or historical figures, all exude their own energy. Consider whether this is positive or negative.

Disturbing pictures should be avoided. Distorted faces, or the faces of the legendary demons and villains of comic books and scary movies are a big 'no' to have in the home. If you do include them, you are bringing in negative energy. I don't even like to have DVDs of frightening movies in my home and I never allowed my child to watch them. They leave an imprint of negative energy on the mind.

## Include happy and inspiring people

Try to include images of only genuinely happy faces in your home, or choose portraits of people who inspire you. These emanate positive energy. The best examples of uplifting pictures are holy images such as portraits or paintings of Jesus, the Madonna or Buddha. These holy pictures exude a pure, beautiful energy that gives your home a revitalizing serenity and positive chi.

# 30 Chipped crockery brings bad luck

There is little more annoying, or worse luck, than drinking coffee from a chipped cup or eating one's dinner from a cracked plate. Chinese matriarchs consider damaged crockery a bad omen and, no matter how costly the piece, throw it away. When you drink from a chipped cup, or eat from a cracked plate, you introduce broken energy into your system. Bad luck, or loss, comes instantly!

Should you ever be served tea or coffee in a chipped cup do not drink from it as you will be drawing bad luck to you. Instead, decline the drink politely.

## Clearing out your cupboards

Look through your cupboards carefully, and throw away any chipped or cracked cups, glasses, bowls and plates. Even if the crack is just a hairline one, it is best to throw away the piece. This clear out is an excellent opportunity to create positive chi. Ensure the insides of your cupboards are dust-free, and place your unblemished crockery and glassware in order.

By ensuring all the crockery in your home is in perfect condition, you are encouraging good luck.

# Dispelling yin energy from antique furniture   31

Think carefully before installing antique furniture in your home, and especially inside your bedroom. If you sleep on an old, antique bed you run the danger of absorbing the left-over energy of previous occupants while you sleep.

If you do have antique beds and cabinets, wipe the furniture thoroughly with rock salt or sea salt. This will help eliminate any bad vibrations that may be stuck on the furniture. Usually the harder the wood, the denser it is, allowing hundreds of years of old energy to be ingrained in it.

The old energy may be positive but, if it is bad, then you are sure to be affected. In any case, old furniture always has lots of yin energy. It is therefore always best to cleanse your antique furniture. If you haven't yet done so, it is not too late. Make sure you clean the inside as well as the outside. Placing a sachet of salt inside old cabinets is also a good idea.

Often beautifully made, antique furniture is a desirable addition to the home so long as it is cleansed of old yin energy and revitalized with new yang energy. Putting such furniture outside – but not in direct sunlight where it could distort or fade – to absorb cosmic yang energy for three days is an excellent idea.

Antique furniture is full of yin energy, which can have you falling asleep at your desk. Cleanse it with rock salt to create positive yang energy and good concentration as you work.

## ENERGY TIP

### Cleansing with rock salt

Always cleanse antique furniture of other people's energy. To clear old, possibly negative, energy use rock salt rubbed gently over the surface. Imagine that the salt is drawing out all adverse energy as you work. If bad energy has been introduced to your home via the antique furniture, you will notice that tension starts to dissolve once the furniture is cleansed. Any harmful emotions such as hostility or anger will be very much reduced. Everyone living in your home will feel the positive benefits of this powerful cleansing ritual.

# Chapter Two

# Secrets of Feng Shui Energy

Having plentiful, positive energy in your home is vital to your well-being – energy levels are affected by the combination of yin and yang, the inclusion of positive elements and the beneficial use of colour. If you can follow the simple rules governing their use, you will be well on the way to receiving their positive benefits.

Always remember that chi energy is around us and our homes all the time, so it is essential to learn to harness it and make it work for you. None of the tips is complicated – indeed the most worthwhile require no more than an understanding of the positive power of space and the importance of keeping your main rooms clear of the clutter of life.

These Tips will successfully enhance the energy of your home, while giving you a solid basis on which to build the rest of your feng shui knowledge.

# Good-energy people live in good-energy homes 32

Good-energy homes are those where both the space itself and everything in it, including the people who occupy it, exude balanced and vibrant energy. Feng shui offers guidelines for creating this harmony of spatial and human energy, and for ensuring a good mix of male and female energies.

## Balancing your home energy

A harmony of yin and yang, female and male energy, in the home is desirable. The secret lies in understanding the essence of yin and yang, as harmony does not necessarily rely on equal amounts of both. For vitality, action, and success in our pursuits, we need yang energy, but for rest, spirituality and inner power we need yin energy. A good-energy home reflects this balance of yin and yang.

## The effects of too much yin energy

As a general rule there should not be an excess of yin symbols in the home. This happens when the colour scheme and décor appear resoundingly feminine, with excessive use of all the yin colours which tend to be dark, sombre and cold. This is not conducive to

growth and development. Dark-coloured paintings and dimmed lighting through the house are thus to be avoided. Rooms should not be too cold, and there should not be a complete absence of sounds and music. When yin energy dominates, precious yang energy gets suppressed. Excessively yin homes also suffer acutely from a lack of the male essence.

If women occupy such a house or apartment, they will find it difficult to have a successful relationship with a man. If men live here they will find it hard to get started on their projects. Success can be elusive. When there is an imbalance of yin and yang, social life becomes non-existent. And when a married couple occupies a home with unbalanced energy, there will be less likelihood of success and opportunities because the feng shui is out of sync.

Homes with positive energy tend to have a lot of yang elements, including vibrant colours, happy sounds and appropriate warmth.

Yin energy can be soothing, particularly in a bedroom where pale yin colours are used to provide tranquillity. The effect, however, can be overly feminine.

# 33 Secrets of the five elements

One of the great secrets of feng shui in the days before it became a household word was the principle of the five elements: water, wood, fire, earth and metal, These govern much of feng shui's principles. Today the theory of five elements is no longer a secret and many people who follow the Chinese esoteric sciences, including feng shui and fortune telling, the cultural arts such as kung fu and tai chi, as well as Chinese traditional medicine, are familiar with it.

All of these practices were based on the correct application of the five-element theory. The simplicity of this theory lies in the belief that literally everything in the Universe – from smells and tastes to colours, shapes, numbers, musical notes, directions, trigrams, symbols, seasons, body parts and organs, and so on – belongs to one of the five elements.

## Harmonizing energy in your home

Assessing every item in your home according to whether it is water, wood, fire, earth or metal will allow you to get a feel for which elements dominate your home. This is the key to assessing your home's energy harmony. If you want to create powerful feng shui in the energy of your living space, then understanding the cycles and attributes of the five elements is the first step. Even people – based on their birth data and gender – can be defined according to these elements.

## The five-element cycle

Assessing how the five elements are represented in your home helps you to understand its energy. The attributes of the five elements balance one another as shown below.

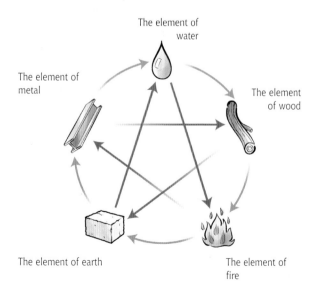

The element of water

The element of metal

The element of wood

The element of earth

The element of fire

Water

Plants represent the wood element

Earth

The metal element

# Use the correct element colours for important rooms 34

Colour is one of the easiest ways to bring harmonious energy into your living space. You can increase the power of feng shui in your home using the 'Later Heaven Pa Kua'. Almost all yang feng shui formulas depend on this arrangement of trigrams with eight sides. These reflect the eight compass directions, as well as their corresponding element and trigram. From these two attributes – element and trigram – it is possible to allocate different colours to each part of the home. The 'Pa Kua' also helps you to use the most effective combinations of colours to enhance the energy in the most important rooms of your home.

The illustration shows which growth and resource colours (see the chart below) should be used at the different compass directions to gain your home the most beneficial effect.

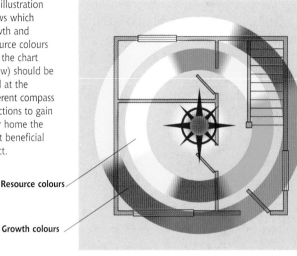

Resource colours

Growth colours

## Using a compass

Stand at the centre of your home and use a compass to find your orientations. By thinking of your home as one big space, you can mentally place the different rooms of your house into the sectors which equate to particular directions.

The important rooms of your home are your bedroom, your foyer area where the main door is placed, your dining room, your kitchen, your work/study area and your living room. Depending on your lifestyle, different rooms will carry different connotations for you so you must also go with your own feelings when placing emphasis on rooms. For example, if you work from home and spend your day in your work/study area, it will be of particular significance to you.

## Table of elements and colours for different room locations

| Room location | Room element | Yin or Yang | Shade of colour | Growth colour | Resource colour | Killing colour | Exhausting colour |
|---|---|---|---|---|---|---|---|
| **North** | WATER | Yang | Darker | **WHITE** | **BLUE** | YELLOW | GREEN |
| **South** | FIRE | Yin | Lighter | **BROWN** | **RED** | WHITE | EARTH |
| **East** | WOOD | Yang | Darker | **BLUE** | **GREEN** | WHITE | RED |
| **West** | METAL | Yin | Lighter | **YELLOW** | **WHITE** | RED | YELLOW |
| **CENTRE** | EARTH | Both | Both | **RED** | **YELLOW** | GREEN | WHITE |
| **Southeast** | WOOD | Yin | Lighter | **BLUE** | **GREEN** | WHITE | RED |
| **Northwest** | METAL | Yang | Darker | **YELLOW** | **WHITE** | RED | YELLOW |
| **Southwest** | EARTH | Yin | Lighter | **RED** | **YELLOW** | GREEN | WHITE |
| **Northeast** | EARTH | Yang | Darker | **RED** | **YELLOW** | GREEN | WHITE |

## Yang and yin shades of colour

To boost the energy in your important rooms with colour therapy, be aware of yang and yin. The more white added to a colour the more yang it becomes, while the darker the shade, the more yin it will be. Use the table shown above to choose the overall colour scheme for each room in your home, and to decide on particular shades.

# 35 Be sensitive to element clashes in your rooms

If light, bright yang shades dominate a room, incorporate accents of darker yin shades for an harmonious energy balance.

It is advisable to also take note of the killing and exhausting colours that will harm the energy of a room. Killing colours create element clashes that cause the energy to turn unstable and weak, thereby becoming negative. The way to tell if the colour scheme of a room clashes with its intrinsic energy is to check the Table of elements and colours for different room locations (see Tip 34). This enables you to determine what colours and colour combinations to avoid.

Clashing colours, whether on the walls, curtains or carpets, in important rooms are deemed to be harmful. When colours are out of sync it is best to give your room a makeover – you will feel the difference in energy instantly.

## Using colour therapy

It is easy to implement colour therapy in feng shui but it is important to take note of whether rooms need to be darker or brighter. By developing sensitivity to the shades of colours, you will become aware of their yin or yang nature.

Sometimes you can get the colours right but still get the yin and yang essence wrong. To create the most conducive energy for the room, give the shades of colours as much attention as the colours themselves. For instance there are many shades and gradations of red and it is vital to use the right shade when creating the colour scheme for, say, a bedroom. In this case, as the colour of the bedroom should not be too overpowering, tone down the shade of red if necessary.

At the same time think about whether colours complement the yin or yang essence of the room. Remember that when the room is said to be yin, it is advisable to create a balance by incorporating some yang shades, and vice versa.

Clashing colours disturb the energy of a room, destabilizing it so that it becomes harmful.

For this earth room with a yang essence, warm cream furnishings balance deep red walls.

# Three dynamite colour combinations 36

As well as the element colours, think about using some of the special colour combinations. These fall outside the standard element analysis of colours but are beneficial for other reasons. The following three colour combinations are recommended as being particularly auspicious.

## Black and white

The epitome of the yin and yang symbol is the combination of black and white. Black is yin while white is yang so the combination of these two colours is an expression of the perfect Universe where everything is properly balanced. Thus, contrary to some conventional thinking, the black and white look is very good feng shui. This look is very popular amongst those who prefer the minimalist school of decoration – minimal can also be auspicious!

## Red and gold

This combination possesses imperial attributes. Red is the colour which reigns supreme as the ultimate auspicious colour. Its attributes of strength and good fortune reflect its yang essence and it is believed to signify the upward-flowing energy that reflects the fire element. Red is embraced as a lucky colour that is suitable for all 'happiness' occasions, celebrations and festivities. So every corner of the house can benefit from red. Use red with care in bedrooms, though, as – unless toned down – it can be too yang for sleeping.

When gold is added to red, the combination brings protective safeguards. Red and gold is regarded as a very special and safe colour combination. It has the power to overcome all negative tangible energy that is brought by annual afflictions and bad flying stars. Red and gold are also the cardinal remedial colours of feng shui.

The combination of red and gold, with its yang essence, boosts revitalizing energy in the home and protects against harmful energy.

## Purple and silver

This is the combination that brings money and increased profits, and it is especially popular amongst those who understand the Cantonese dialect. When the words purple and silver are put together in Cantonese they sound like 'ngan chee', or money. Purple is also the colour of the completion star and the colour of wealth. Silver, being metal, produces water the colour of purple. Being a symbol of wealth has enhanced the popularity of this colour combination, which is especially suitable for a northwest-facing room.

Purple and silver combine to bring wealth.

# 37    Decoding the meanings of shapes

There are five basic shapes that influence the energy of spaces and these arise from their element associations.

• The **round** shape is very popular as it signifies gold (metal element).

• The **square** shape signifies relationships and the family unit (earth element).

• The **rectangle** shape signifies growth energy (wood element).

• The **triangular** shape signifies upward mobility (fire element).

• The **curvilinear** shape signifies fluidity (water element).

When you think about shapes, consider the layout of your home as well as the shape of individual rooms. To ensure a symmetry of energy, feng shui always favours regular as opposed to irregular shapes. Symmetry and balance are central concepts in feng shui so that, for a shape to be irregular or asymmetrical, implies that it is incomplete. Thus a full square is always better than one with a corner missing. Rectangles that are well proportioned are preferable to ones that are too narrow, which also suggests that part of the shape is missing.

A full circle is preferable to a half circle, which is why bay windows are inadvisable. Small irregularities in the corners of rooms cause irregularity of luck. The 'Pa Kua' – and octagon – is also considered an auspicious shape, especially when used for dining and coffee tables.

Paint walls to emphasize the regularity of room shapes. **Rectangular** walls, which are higher than they are broad – without appearing incomplete – are particularly beneficial in east and southeast corners of the home since the shape here signifies growth and success. The rectangle is the shape of the wood element and wood suggests spring, the season of growth.

Perfectly **square** shapes, which belong to the earth element, are ideal for the dining room and the dining table since the earth element not only reflects the stability of grounding energy, it also stands for the mother. The energy of the square is balanced and auspicious for continued family harmony.

**Round** shapes denote the metal element and are suitable for the west and northwest. A perfect round patch created with clever paintwork on a northwest wall brings good luck to the family patriarch. Paint it in gold for lustre and extra good-luck symbolism. Do not make it too large, though, since the round shape can be overpowering.

## Making the most of your home's layout

Although regular shapes are better feng shui, many homes have some irregularities – such as a 'missing' corner or a bay window. Still, there is much you can do to promote harmonious energy in your home by incorporating regular, auspicious shapes wherever possible.

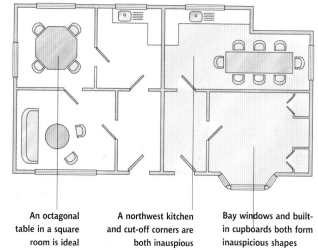

An octagonal table in a square room is ideal

A northwest kitchen and cut-off corners are both inauspious

Bay windows and built-in cupboards both form inauspicious shapes

# Keeping rooms clean and uncluttered 38

Living spaces have a tendency to get cluttered; it is as if the mere act of living creates instant chaos. Observe a hotel room on arrival, and then again a day after you have been staying in it, and you will get a feel for just how easy it is for space to become littered with daily clutter.

## Removing the obstacles

Good energy in a room gets insidiously corrupted as this kind of clutter builds up over time. It is for this reason that I encourage everyone to have enough storage space in their homes and to develop a 'neat and tidy' mindset. This is vital, because clutter creates instant obstacles. It blocks the flow of energy in the living space without you realizing it. If the corner that is becoming filled with old newspapers and magazines happens to be an important corner from a feng shui perspective – perhaps it has all your auspicious stars for the year – or if the space getting piled up with unwanted stuff is a major conduit area of the house, the effect on your wellbeing is bound to be negative.

## Clearing your workspace

I have undertaken many consultations in which the only problem I encountered blocking the luck of my clients was an incredible pile-up of clutter in their workspace. As soon as I told them to clear the room to let in new energy, they immediately experienced better luck. So do be alert to clutter, and clear it out on a regular basis before it accumulates.

A clean, tidy workspace allows the free flow of fresh energy. If you start letting your workspace become cluttered, revitalizing energy will get blocked.

**ENERGY TIP**

## Weekly clean-up

Make sure that clutter doesn't build up in your home by clearing it out every week. Common offenders are old newspapers and magazines, as well as pairs of shoes. Tidy away shoes and throw away paper rubbish.

Clear out clutter     Keep rooms dirt-free

# 39 Creating space in the right places

The first step in creating a harmonious place in which to live is to define the space itself so that chi flows unimpeded into the home and settles and accumulates in auspicious areas. You need to create the best routes and resting places for the energy to move and gather. If your home has become overcrowded with too much furniture, the removal of even a single piece can make all the difference.

It is a good idea to begin by taking stock of the overall arrangement of cupboards, chairs and tables in your living space. This snapshot overview enables you to see how each room could benefit from having some space freed up to encourage good-fortune energy to settle in all the right places of the home.

*Thoughtful spacing of objects in your living space provides chi with resting places and routes through which to move unimpeded.*

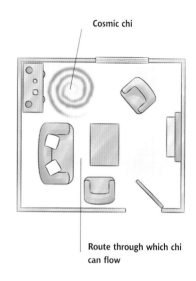

**Cosmic chi**

**Route through which chi can flow**

In a living room, chi gathers in an empty space diagonally across from the door before it flows into other parts of the living space.

## Attracting cosmic chi

Most often the best place to create some empty space for the chi to settle is deep inside a room. In the living area, for instance, the best place for chi to collect is the corner diagonally opposite the entrance door. This is an auspicious corner so that chi settling here before moving into other parts of the home will also be auspicious. To enhance the corner further after de-cluttering it, place just one lucky object here – cosmic chi will respond positively to its presence.

# Arranging furniture to create a flow of chi 40

Creating 'chi pathways' is as important as having oases of auspicious chi in the different rooms of your home. Chi pathways are invisible conduits of energy created by the strategic placement of furniture.

The flow of chi inside the home should take on a meandering character because chi that moves slowly tends to be a lot more auspicious than chi that moves too fast. Inside the home, no matter how small the space, try creating 'pathways' with your eyes. Chi almost always follows the same routes that people take when walking around at home, so the pathways should be easy to visualize.

## Avoiding roadblocks

Think about chi pathways when arranging your furniture. If you position it without allowing space for a meandering flow of chi, you will miss out on the harmonious energy and luck it can bring. Perhaps worse still, you might have placed a roadblock on your success path so that you keep meeting dead ends.

The ideal way to arrange furniture is to do so with an eye to allowing energy to flow seamlessly from one room to the next without you even being too aware of it.

Visualize the chi pathways in your living space. Make sure you are clear about how chi will enter the room and how it will travel to other rooms. You may want to leave doors open to encourage the flow.

The more spacious your home, the easier it will be to create chi pathways. However, even in the smallest living space it's important that there are routes for chi to move freely around furniture and from room to room.

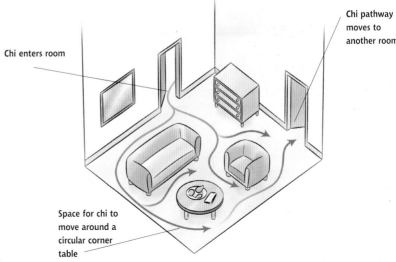

Chi enters room

Chi pathway moves to another room

Space for chi to move around a circular corner table

# 41 The layout of rooms determines the energy flow

The way rooms are used and allocated within an existing layout also has a powerful effect on how energy flows and settles in the home. To make the best of your home feng shui make sure that your busy rooms, where most of your activity takes place, are not all focused in one corner of the house, leaving other parts of the home deserted or underused.

The key to good feng shui is to ensure that energy flows throughout the whole house and not just to certain well-used corners. If there is a room, or rooms, that rarely get used, think about how the space might become more functional and inviting.

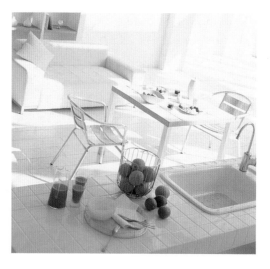

An open-plan kitchen and living room has cooking, eating and sitting areas. This layout creates a good balance of energy across the whole space, with no area likely to become neglected.

# 42 Keeping a room as a private inner sanctum

Do draw a line between the private and public areas of your home. Irrespective of the size of your home, demarcate a special area, or areas, that remain out of bounds to visitors. The inner sanctum of a home is where the energy can be a little more yin. Here, with the help of yin energy, the wealth of the home is allowed to accumulate.

## Protecting your wealth

One of the most potent feng shui secrets is a private space in the home where the family's wealth vase, among other feng shui enhancing symbols, is kept. This private space is usually an inner area, or an inner room, on the highest floor of the house and not accessible to visitors. The presence of such a room in your home – and you can designate your bedroom as your inner sanctum if there is no other suitable space – is also where you can create an altar. This may be for yourself or your family, and provides a sacred place for lucky objects with uplifting associations.

# Keeping the energy of rooms dynamic from year to year   43

During my years in Hong Kong, when I rubbed shoulders with many of the then colony's wealthiest families and their matriarchs, I picked up another secret of the most successful Taoist practitioners. Each year, just before the lunar new year, it is exceedingly good luck to welcome in a new piece of furniture, or a large enhancing object such as a new set of the health, wealth and prosperity deities Fuk Luk Sau, a new wealth God or a new vase – anything that is noticeable and affects the chi energy of the room.

## Out with the old, in with the new

This introduction of one new signature piece should be accompanied by the removal of

The new object you bring into your home need not be expensive – it could be a simple bowl in a shape and colour that enhances the energy of a room.

another piece. This could be an old sofa, an old table, an old statue or an old vase.

The act of bringing in one new piece and removing one old decorative item or piece of furniture causes the chi to be symbolically replenished. In this way, the energy of the room rejuvenates from year to year.

I have been carrying out an 'out with the old, in with the new' policy every year since the late Eighties with great success. I truly believe that this is what has made my house literally 'grow' before my eyes. It just gets bigger and

better every year! I remember in those early days when I first came back to live in my house after returning from Hong Kong, my house was small and modest. Today, after many layers of renovations, my house is big, sprawling and spacious – some eight times the size.

## Lucky objects

Think carefully about the new object you bring into your home each year. The practice provides a great opportunity to accumulate items with lucky or uplifting properties.

# Chapter Three

# Firing Up Your Living Spaces

Once you have completed the basics you can prepare each room to benefit most effectively from feng shui cures.

Every part of the home – from the garden, through the front door, and into every room of the house – can be enhanced with feng shui cures. Water, light and symbolic guardians each play their part in empowering the energy, while the auspicious placement of furniture and decorations will clear any blocked energy pathways and charge the positive nature of the chi.

Learning the secrets of energizing the chi of a living room while making your bedroom a restful haven will give you the opportunity to make your home a refuge against the problems of the outside world.

# Empowering the main door    44

The main door of your home is where the powerful cosmic energy of the outer environment connects with and enters your home. All other doorways, entrances and exits are secondary conduits of chi. It is very beneficial to pay special attention to the main door of the house if you want to enjoy continuous good feng shui.

## Protect and enhance your entrance

While there are lots of ways to encourage good chi to enter through the main door of your home, all can be summarized in just two words – 'protect' and 'enhance'. Most importantly, keep the foyer areas inside and outside well lit. If you can, it is also beneficial to display auspicious images near the vicinity of the door to empower it.

## Traditional screening wall

In the old days the wealthy Chinese used to place a screening wall about three metres (ten feet) from the door, facing it. On this screening wall, they placed images of auspicious creatures, such as Gods of wealth, the nine dragons, or bright red peonies associated with the eight Immortals. All of these auspicious images were believed to attract fresh new cosmic chi into the home continuously.

You can employ the essence of this method near your own main door – perhaps including auspicious features in a front garden – referring to the plan opposite for ideas.

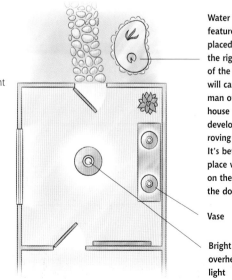

The main doors of domestic dwellings and businesses need brightly lit entrances to create good fortune feng shui.

• Water is a powerful energizing element in a front garden.
• Vases create peace and harmony on an otherwise uncluttered side table.
• Bright lights encourage a flow of good chi to enter the home.

Water feature placed on the right side of the door will cause the man of the house to develop a roving eye. It's better to place water on the left of the door

Vase

Bright overhead light

# 45 Feeding the growth energy at doorways with water

*Water within a living space is extremely auspicious.*

One of the most powerful ways to boost the energy of your main door so that replenishing cosmic energy is always encouraged to enter the home is to place water close by. The presence of water, when located either inside or outside the home, promotes what is known as growth energy. In the language of feng shui, 'growth' is used to describe the vital ingredient that brings never-ending good fortune.

### Inside or outside the door?

If you live on landed property it is an excellent idea to dig into the ground just outside the front door. Water sited here creates excellent, expanding good fortune for the house's residents. A pond of at least a metre (about three feet) deep is ideal. Use a filter

to ensure the water stays clean at all times. It will then bring wealth and abundance to the house. You can keep either fish or plants in your pond.

### Water features in flats

If you live in a flat, check if it's possible to place a water feature just inside the entrance door. Position it so that it faces the door from about three metres (ten feet) away. Preferably, for the best flow of chi, it should be located to the right of the door when looking in from the outside. If your flat is small, use a small water feature such as the six-tier waterfall with three 'peaks' which I designed specially for this purpose. Alternatively, a vase filled with fresh water will also be effective.

---

## ENERGY TIP

### Where to place water

Water can be placed inside or outside a main door. Outdoors, you don't need an elaborate fountain – an urn of water is fine, as long as the water is clean. Bird baths are also good feng shui, but they must be placed to the left of the main door when you are standing at the threshold looking out, otherwise infidelity may result!

# Creating good energy on both sides of the door  46

Creating an accumulation of good energy on both sides of the main front door is incredibly beneficial. Keep the foyer areas inside and outside the door free of clutter and clean at all times. If the door, or any surrounding object, gets broken, becomes faulty, or starts to peel, repair it or repaint it immediately. The presence of water nearby is excellent but, to further enhance the good energy, place your guardian protectors in brass or ceramic around the main door. Growing plants in pots outside the door also creates revitalizing energy.

## Five-element energy

The aim is to create a pool of five-element energy – the presence of all five elements symbolizing a universe of good energy. Thus water

brings a flow of wealth, fire brings success and recognition, metal brings protection and strength, earth brings grounding luck, and wood brings growth and expansion. Use your creativity to work at creating this pool of five-element energy, both inside as well as outside the door.

If you have French doors leading from your living room into the garden, consider what is directly outside the doors. Dead plants or clutter outside affects the feng shui inside, so keep both areas clean and fresh.

Something as simple as a bowl of hyacinths brings the elements of earth (the soil) and wood (the flowering bulbs) to a space. You could even use a metal container for a third element.

# 47 Secondary doors that support the main door

While focusing attention on the main door, do not forget the secondary doors that allow entry into your home. The best are those that 'support' the main door.

Flats usually have a maximum of two entrance doors – the main door and a back door. Houses, however, can have several secondary doors, including doors that open into the house from the garage, as well as sliding side doors that lead into gardens. A secondary door is best located in the northwest, or facing

Main door        Secondary door

## What is a secondary door?

A secondary door is any door that leads out from the main structure of the home. Secondary doors include those that open onto garages, back yards or gardens. Even if you use these secondary doors infrequently, they still have a powerful impact on the feng shui of your home.

Some dwellings have secondary doors that are also positioned at the front of the home. The secondary door is the one you use least frequently.

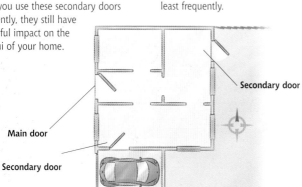

Secondary door

Main door

Secondary door

in that direction, where it will attract powerful good luck to your home from Heaven.

## Enhancing the main door's energy

The position of the secondary door should support the energy of the main door. For example, if the main door is located in the south, then a secondary door located in the east or southeast would strengthen the main door considerably, bringing success luck. However, a secondary door in the north weakens the energy of the main door, even if you have followed good feng shui practice around it.

To find out the best position for secondary doors in relation to the main door, refer to the table.

## Check out your door locations

| Main door location | Beneficial secondary door | Harmful secondary door |
| --- | --- | --- |
| NORTH | NORTHWEST, WEST | SOUTHWEST, NORTHEAST |
| SOUTH | SOUTHEAST, EAST | NORTH |
| EAST | NORTH | NORTHWEST, WEST |
| WEST | SOUTHWEST, NORTHEAST | SOUTH |
| SOUTHWEST | SOUTH | SOUTHEAST, EAST |
| SOUTHEAST | NORTH | NORTHWEST, WEST |
| NORTHWEST | SOUTHWEST, NORTHEAST | SOUTH |
| NORTHEAST | SOUTH | SOUTHEAST, EAST |

# Keeping the main door fully energized    48

Creating good energy around and near the main door is the first step in ensuring that only good energy enters the home. It is also beneficial to keep track of the changing energy patterns that afflict the main door from year to year.

## Protective metal

Usually the presence of metal energy in the form of celestial guardians, such as a brass Chi Lin or brass Fu dogs, flanking the door offers strong protection against afflictive energies. It is also useful to install feng shui cures around the vicinity of the main door to ensure that your good feng shui is protected from year to year.

## Good-fortune locations

First use a compass to locate the direction of the main door, then check the energy of this location for the coming year.

In 2007, for example, you will have enjoyed good fortune if your main door is located in the southwest, and it was brightly lit – this is because good fortune in the southwest is enhanced by bright lighting. However, if your door is located in the northwest, you may have suffered misfortune where the afflictive star caused quarrelsome energy, resulting in family arguments and conflict. In 2008, the good-fortune location for the main door moves to the east sector, and in 2009, good luck flies to the southeast sector of the home.

As such good-fortune locations and areas of affliction change from year to year, always be prepared to update your feng shui. Remember that these energy changes begin at the start of the lunar New Year, on February 4. You will always find up-to-date information at www.wofs.com, which also carries an analysis of the annual changes in energy patterns that affect your main door.

A brass Fu dog flanking the main door acts as a guardian against harmful energy.

# 49 Installing symbolic door guardians

One of the easiest ways to protect your main door against tangible and intangible afflictive energies is to do what the Chinese do – install celestial guardians each side of the main door. This symbolic gesture is second nature to the Chinese and part of their cultural tradition.

Having celestial guardians just outside the home's main entrance is excellent protection against bad people, bad spirits and bad luck. It is one of the most powerful pratices of feng shui. Most important is the protection against bad people who would otherwise bring afflictive energies into the home.

Potent protectors of a property's main door, Fu dogs should be identical and flank each side of the door to give equal protection. Keep them in pristine condition.

Fu dogs outside an ancient temple in China carry symbolic barrels designating wealth and protection.

## Firing up the main door

The presence of protectors fires up the main door with a special energy, particularly if they are celestial creatures. The Chinese usually ask a Taoist priest to perform a ritual to 'open the eyes' of their celestial guardians, but I have found that they perform just as well with or without such a ritual. If you regard them as your protectors, they will take on this role empowered by the strength of your belief.

## Every year is different!

Bad luck comes in many forms – including loss, illness and accidents – and the Chinese Almanac lists over 250 different types of afflictive stars that 'fly' to various locations from year to year. It is impossible to keep track of all of these afflictive stars, and it is not necessary to do so. The Chinese purchase the Chinese Almanac, or Tung Shu, each year to discover where and when negative afflictions will affect their doors and homes so that they can employ timely protection.

Different parts of your home, inside and out, take turns to be lucky and unlucky year by year – feng shui is dynamic so nothing remains constant. While it shouldn't be a problem to live with minor afflictions, do not ignore any major ones.

Most afflictions are easily remedied with five-element and symbolic 'cures' – see Tips 46 and 133. You can use these to strengthen the power of the celestial protectors by the door. If you are going through a spate of bad luck, it is definitely worth checking the whereabouts of this year's afflictions. Once you have installed the remedies you need, you should notice a change in fortune.

# Celestial protectors create a strong defence 50

To protect your main door with celestial guardians, first decide which ones you prefer. Three of the most popular, employed by the Chinese for centuries, are Fu dogs, Pi Yaos and Chi Lins. These guardians are described as celestial because, like the dragon, they are not seen in this world. Their appearance seems to be a fusion of various creatures, and many believe these heavenly protectors to be powerful enough to ward off evil people and harmful energy.

## Using three protectors

Personally I use all three of these celestial protectors as I am lucky to have a large house with many entrances and doors. For my main door I use a giant pair of brass phoenixes – known for bringing in new opportunities – and, for my secondary doors, I use Pi Yao (dragon dog) and Chi Lin (dragon horse). I am especially fond of the Pi Yao, which is a remedy against one of the most afflictive annual stars, the Tai Sui, or Grand Duke Jupiter. The Pi Yao is also a bringer of great wealth! The Chi Lin protects against the afflictive stars, the three killings, which otherwise bring loss.

The dragon, a symbol of courage, is a powerful protector in the home.

# Invoking the shielding spirit of animals 51

Red ribbons stimulate the power of protective animal guardians.

If you wish you can also install other kinds of guardian protectors, perhaps those from your own culture – the Balinese, for example, have their own fierce-looking protectors, and even special designs for their doors. You can choose wild animals known for their fierce protective instincts – perhaps the lion, tiger, rhino, elephant or leopard. Friends of mine have used life-sized statues of tigers, elephants and lions to great effect.

## Activate your guardians

Your own protectors will have more power if you observe a couple of rituals. Firstly, place the animal guardians outside your home so that they flank the doorway and look outwards. Secondly, activate these guardians by tying red ribbons – if possible, use a mystical knot – around their necks. This will energize the animal guardians and strengthen their power. The Taoists believe that, once these rituals have been performed, the guardians are imbued with the protector spirit of the Cosmos, enabling them to guard your home with much greater efficiency.

# 52 Clearing blockages in the hallway

It is all too easy for clutter such as packages, newspapers, junk mail, raincoats, umbrellas and so on to accumulate in the foyer area of your home. This is really the worst place to let clutter pile up, and it can happen so fast that you may only notice it when you start to look for reasons why your luck has suddenly taken a turn for the worse.

*Bright, clean halls and foyers create excellent feng shui, allowing chi to meander and bring the inhabitants good fortune. When chi becomes inhibited due to clutter, misfortune can result.*

## Reversals of fortune

Frequently, I have gone to the homes of people who have suffered sudden reversals of fortune only to discover that the downturn in their lives or businesses has been caused by nothing more sinister that a blockage of energy. This blockage is usually near the main door, though

sometimes it occurs in corners that would be bringing annual luck were it not for the piles of clutter suppressing the good fortune.

## Forming good habits

Make it a habit to keep the area just inside the home, as well as just outside the main door, clear of blockages. Keep plants and any other decorative objects in good condition, and don't let too many pile up.

*It's fine to have some furniture in your hall to slow down chi, but don't let clutter pile up – display only a few decorative items.*

# Creating feng shui strength in living rooms    53

The living room area is probably the best place to activate good feng shui by using symbolic decorative images. One of the joys of feng shui is that there are so many animals, flowers and other images available that are deemed to have an auspicious meaning.

## Activating the eight aspirations

We all have many hopes and desires, and the Chinese have summarized them into eight main aspirations, as follows:

1  A loving and close family

2  Attaining career success

3  Good descendants

4  A good and respectable name

5  Enjoying good health

6  Knowledge and wisdom

7  Wealth

8  The protection of a powerful mentor.

Each of these eight types of good fortune can be activated and strengthened using symbolic images that will enhance good feng shui. Images of auspicious animals have appeared in paintings, sculptures, porcelain, embroidery and carvings throughout the history of Chinese culture. This belief in lucky imagery has resulted in the wealth of wonderful decorative art we have inherited today from hundreds of years of Chinese artistry.

## Auspicious objects create good chi

Simply decorating the living room with auspicious objects will usually create the chi

Animal images, such as the horse, are symbols of strength and good fortune.

energy that attracts the eight types of good fortune. Use the living room to showcase art and decorative objects featuring auspicious images, making sure that they are correctly placed to enhance the feng shui.

## Positioning art for positive benefits

Thoughtful positioning is particularly vital if you are siting decorative objects in corners of the room. Here, each object should reflect the element of the corner.

For example, in an earth corner of the southwest or northeast you might want to put an earth-based object such as a ceramic or crystal figurine of an auspicious animal. Remember that the luckiest corner is always diagonally opposite the door.

If you hang up a mirror on a wall in the living room, make sure that it does not reflect the door – otherwise it will cause chi energy to fly out immediately.

# 54 Bright light always generates yang energy

As well as using art and decorative objects in the home to bring good luck, you can also harness the powerful yang energy of bright lights. A home is always luckier when the ambience is bright, without being glaring, than when it is sombre.

Be sensitive to the moods created in your home by light. Soft or warm lighting – or indeed any kind of lighting that creates the ambience you feel most comfortable with – is fine so long as your home is never overly dark with lots of shadows. In the daytime your home will flood with the stimulating yang energy of the sun but, at nighttime, the darker, cooler yin energy from moonlight sets in.

### Yin-yang balance at nighttime

While yin chi is suitable for the nocturnal hours, keep a good amount of yang energy flowing through your home as well. Remember that in yin there must always be a little bit of yang, and vice versa, as an excess of one or the other results in space that is not in balance and so cannot attract good fortune. This is why keeping the lights turned on through the night is such a good feng shui habit to develop.

In my home I keep the garden and porch lights on, while inside the house my altar lights and living room downlights stay on as well. My main door foyer area is always kept lit as this part of the home benefits most from a continuous supply of yang chi energy.

# 55 Let natural sounds permeate your living areas

If you don't have animals to keep the atmosphere full of good yang energy, invest in pairs of dog or cat figurines as yang symbols.

The sounds of nature are a wonderful source of yang energy. Silent homes or rooms – suggesting the yin aura of tombs and underground places – are not at all conducive to activity and life. For homes to resonate with good feng shui, create features that emit natural sounds. The best include the sound of water flowing gently through a water feature, the sound of twinkling windchimes, or the rustle of leaves blown by fans.

### When the home is empty all day

If the home stays silent through the daytime, especially when the whole family is out – perhaps husband and wife at work and kids at school – the atmosphere within will take on yin essence unless there is the sound of life. I am a great believer in keeping a pair of pet dogs or cats as these create 'life essence' in the house. Alternatively, a workable solution is to keep the radio or television on while you are away from home.

# Create meandering flows of chi in your home     56

When you arrange the furniture of your home create a mental image of traffic flow – how people will walk around objects – in your mind. Direct the traffic flow by placing pieces of heavy furniture in strategic places. Make sure the flow is meandering, and that family members will not be prone to walking into obstacles or corners. Disarm any sharp edges by placing softer items such as plants and sofas near them.

### Softening the flow in strategic places

When more than two doors form a row where the flow of chi might gather pace, soften the flow by placing sideboards strategically so that the energy flows around them.

For a long corridor in the home, break the flow of energy by placing lights and decorative objects along its length. For a bedroom at the end of a long passageway, soften and slow down the flow of chi using lights and leafy plants.

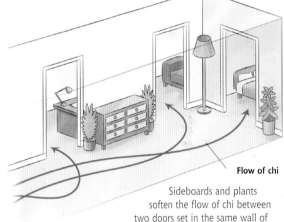

**ENERGY TIP**

### Visualizing flow

Place furniture, lighting and plants to encourage the flow of chi to keep moving along passageways – but not too fast.

**Flow of chi**

Sideboards and plants soften the flow of chi between two doors set in the same wall of this corridor.

# Generate pockets of concentrated energy     57

Create 'pockets' of yang chi energy in every room and you will have good feng shui throughout the home. These pockets are special areas in which people sit and chat, eat or engage in their favourite hobbies regularly so that a concentration of energy builds up. In the living room you will need to arrange the furniture to create a pocket of yang chi whereas in the dining room this is usually formed naturally by meeting around the dining table.

The centre of the house benefits most from a concentration of yang energy. If you find that this is not easily achieved in your home, place a television in the central room to generate a lively ambience. You want the heart of your home to be pulsating, alive and active.

Seating areas naturally attract pockets of positive yang chi.

**Chi pockets**

# 58  Rearrange your décor at frequent intervals

One of the simplest yet most effective feng shui secrets I picked up many years ago when I lived and worked in Hong Kong was the great benefit of regularly rearranging furniture in the home. This encourages chi energy to move, preventing it from becoming stagnant. You do not even have to rearrange the furniture if you like it as it is – just moving it a foot from the wall to give the whole room a good clean then moving it back again will force the chi energy to move.

Rearranging furniture is particularly beneficial because it re-channels the patterns of chi energy, reflecting its dynamic nature and attracting new cosmic energy into your home.

## Annual rearranging and renovation

I usually rearrange my furniture at least once a year. I often move entire sets of furniture from one room to the next, and I even move the pictures hanging on the walls around to different rooms as well. This gives the house a new feel and energy.

I also renovate my house regularly, working on different corners from year to year, making sure that I renovate – in effect, activate – the most auspicious corners for every year. This has given my home a life of its own so that it is forever young and surprising. My husband and I have lived in the same house now for 30 years and it stays as filled with bright energy as it did when it was first built. It has also grown considerably in size.

Feng shui is a dynamic phenomenon and, following this principle, I make sure that nothing in my own home ever stays exactly the same from year to year. As a result my home is regularly recharged with yang energy.

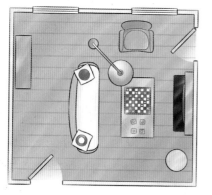

Rearrange furniture in living spaces regularly or, at the least, move it away from the walls and clean thoroughly. Here the table and sofa move opposite the fireplace and the chair and log basket swap positions.

## Observe the renovation taboos every year     59

Regularly carrying out small projects in the auspicious parts of your home will bring great benefits. This is especially true if you live in a house with land attached, or if you live in the country. Every time you activate the lucky corners of your home you will be amazed at how soon you receive some unexpected good fortune. In 2007, for example, the lucky corner of all homes is the southwest corner. If you activate the energy of this corner with building work, or other improvements, you are sure to attract some kind of positive outcome. In 2008 the lucky part of the home is the east and in 2009 it is the southeast.

There are also taboo areas to leave well alone. Renovations or other disturbances in these areas will cause misfortune to befall those living in the house. Visit www.wofs.com to find out the taboo parts of the home for the year you are interested in. For 2007 the taboo sectors, which must be left well alone, are the northeast and the west and, in 2008, the south.

Carrying out renovations, such as giving walls and ceiling a fresh coat of paint, in the auspicious sector of your home for the year brings good luck, but avoid working in taboo areas or your fortunes may change for the worse.

## Bring in daily doses of sun energy     60

This is one of my most popular feng shui tips of all time as it is so easy to practise and brings so much happiness chi into the home. It is an especially effective way to make sure that the family stays together and that all members are blessed by the powerful rejuvenating energy of the sun.

Hang cut crystals of various shapes on windows that catch the rays of the sun directly – in the east during the morning hours and in the west during the afternoon. This breaks down the light of the sun, sending happy rainbow colours into the home. The colours of the rainbow bring in the cosmic power of newly minted energy. Remember that it is far more beneficial to tap morning sunshine energy than afternoon energy because morning energy is young yang, which stays powerful a lot longer to rejuvenate your home.

Always choose bright, sparkling cut crystals, not faded-looking ones. The more glittery a crystal, the more effective it will be at bringing new cosmic energy into your home.

# 61 Dining room mirror doubles abundance

One sure-fire method of ensuring that the family never loses its livelihood, and that the abundance of the home is continually replenished, is to create a 'doubling' effect in the dining room. This is where the family eats its daily meals which, to the Chinese, symbolize sustenance and survival.

Good feng shui is as much about protecting one's rice bowl as it is about creating abundance – though the doubling of food on the table is important. Even very poor families like to make sure that the dining table never looks barren. If possible they prefer it to appear full at every mealtime, an effect often enhanced by a clever layout of dishes. To double this effect, they will often hang a good-sized wall mirror in a strategic position that reflects the food on the table, The good feng shui encourages the family's wealth to grow.

## ENERGY TIP

### Candles bring stimulating yang

Lit candles represent the fire element and are bearers of powerful yang energy to the dining table. To balance and control the fire element here, the candles are placed on a bed of pebbles, which symbolize earth energy. Balanced in this way, the fire energy encourages liveliness in the room.

Placing the wall mirror where it reflects the spread on the table, and all the family members once seated, will encourage a prosperous home.

### Positioning the wall mirror

Firstly, choose a wall mirror that is large enough to suggest wealth and prosperity. A mirror that reflects all family members, as well as the food on the table, is good feng shui. When hanging the mirror in the dining area, make sure that it is not too low. If it does reflect the people in the room make certain that no one's head is inadvertently 'cut off'.

The dining room mirror must not reflect the main door, which causes energizing chi to flow out of the house. It should not reflect any other door, either, or a toilet, a staircase or the kitchen. Whereas food on the table symbolizes livelihood, food that is being prepared or cooked is luck that has not yet ripened. So long as you follow these precautions, the mirror will attract good fortune.

# Golden rules for kitchen location 62

Feng shui gives important guidelines for siting your kitchen. Firstly, it is best located deep inside your home, although not in its centre. If possible, the kitchen should not be visible from the front door so that, ideally, a wall will separate it from the front of the house. It is best sited on the ground floor, as a kitchen located at basement level brings bad luck to the family's matriarch.

As you walk into the home, a kitchen on the right is far preferable to one on the left. Kitchens that are located on the left side of the house, looking in, tend to cause the siblings of the family to quarrel. They can also provoke children to fight severely with their parents.

### Avoid the northwest and southwest

Do not site a kitchen in the northwest of your home as this damages the luck of the patriarch. Often it will cause him to lose his major source of success – be it a powerful benefactor, mentor or patron. A kitchen in the southwest hurts the luck of the matriarch, causing her to

This floor plan shows an ideal location for a kitchen. As you walk in, the kitchen cannot be seen from the front door. It is situated on the ground floor, to the right at the back of the home.

**Kitchen is located at the back of the house to the right**

Front door

lose power and status within the family. In many cases, it causes the husband to take a mistress or even leave the home for a second marriage. Anything that afflicts the matriarch will also cause problems for the family.

# Revitalizing salt rituals in kitchens 63

Of all the rooms in the home, the one most vulnerable to bad or stagnant energy is the kitchen where the family's food is cooked daily. The energy of the kitchen gets transferred easily to the family. Once a year give the floor, door and walls of the kitchen a salt wipe, a simple but powerful way to ensure that kitchen surfaces are clear of negative chi, and that food cooked in your kitchen never gets afflicted by harmful or stagnant energy.

To clean your kitchen with salt, press a damp cloth into natural rock salt and, as you wipe all the surfaces, visualize that you are drawing out the old, negative chi.

Always use natural rock salt because you need the power of the earth – synthetic salt is ineffective.

# 64 Managing fire and water elements

As you wash and cook food in your kitchen, be sensitive to the conflicting energies of the fire and water elements. Of all the elements, fire and water have the potential to be most beneficial or harmful. Water brings wealth but can also drain it away. Fire brings a good name and reputation, attracting honour, fame, success and recognition, but fire can also burn everything down to ashes. Water and fire provide the potential both for very good or very bad outcomes. Between the two, it is water that controls fire.

Inside your kitchen make sure that the water tap is not near the stove and does not directly face it. The stove symbolizes the fire element, which will react negatively to the water element.

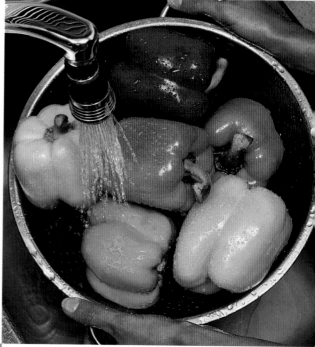

## Locating the sink and stove

Water and fire confrontation is the cause of commotion and quarrels within the home so consider the location of the sink

and stove in your kitchen, and do not have a toilet or water tank above the stove.

During the yin hours of the night, keep at least one light turned on in the kitchen to rekindle the fire energy. Symbolically, this will also keep the kitchen of the home warm, ensuring that yang energy never dies.

### ENERGY TIP

### Siting the stove auspiciously

Avoid putting mirrors or mirror tiles above the stove or they cause the fire energy to double, which is harmful. Also make sure the stove does not face a staircase, refrigerator, toilet, water pipe, store room or door. Ideally, position it diagonally opposite the kitchen door. If it is then opposite a back door, put up a divider to block the energy flowing through the door. The stove should never be below a window.

# Restful energy in the bedroom 65

Always underplay the presence of yang energy when decorating bedrooms. If there is too much yang chi in a bedroom, it will activate your mind and make it difficult for you to sleep well. If yin and yang are not in harmony, this will also result in restlessness. At nighttime, your bedroom signifies a place of security and sanctuary. It's best to choose soothing colours rather than stimulating ones. Neutral colours work a lot better than primary ones.

## Avoid pictures of people

Try not to activate the bedroom with too many decorative objects. Keep celestial guardians and the dragon in the living areas and not the bedroom. It is also best not to hang photographs or paintings of people on bedroom walls. Some newly-weds like to hang their wedding photograph inside the bedroom, but this is definitely not recommended – it is far better to hang your wedding picture in an energizing yang chi area.

## Choose subtle lighting

In the bedroom yin energy should take precedence over yang energy, so keep lighting muted. A general rule is the older a bedroom's occupants, the softer the lighting should be. Lamps are best placed at the sides of the bed, not overhead.

Earth tones such as brown and cream work particularly well in a bedroom because the earth element is grounding and relaxing.

Keep decorative objects to a minimum in the bedroom. The aim is to create a tranquil environment that soothes the mind, allowing deep and restful sleep.

# 66    Cleansing ceremonies in bedrooms

Annually, just before the New Year, give your bedroom, or bedrooms, a thorough symbolic cleansing to remove any stagnating chi that may have accumulated. Give all soft furnishings, including carpets, curtains and bed linens, a good clean. If possible, move furniture so that you can clean the hard-to-get-at places underneath the bed, side tables and cupboards.

## Dispelling negative chi

When you have cleaned the bedroom physically, carry out a cleansing ritual. Firstly, wipe all the surfaces in the bedroom with a cleaning cloth dipped in natural salt water. Then use space-clearing tools such as incense sticks, a metal singing bowl with a wooden mallet, bells and crystals to activate the five elements.

Holding burning incense sticks, walk around the room in a clockwise direction three times, allowing the smoke to symbolically cleanse the room. Repeat the ritual with a singing bowl, noticing how the sounds become lighter as you move around the room. Do the same with a special bell made of seven types of metal. The singing bowl and bell signify the powerful metal element cutting through all illness and misfortune chi. Finish the ritual with the grounding energy of crystals – the best one to use is a single pointed pure quartz crystal to simulate the infinity sign in the air as you walk around the room.

Remember to open your windows and doors when you perform these simple rituals to allow a good flow of chi. It is also beneficial to think happy thoughts as you are performing the cleansing rituals.

## Wood and water chi

Holding a pine branch in one hand and a bowl of water in which you have dissolved natural salt in the other, walk around the bedroom in a clockwise direction. As you walk, dip the pine branch in the salt water and sprinkle it lightly around the room. This symbolizes the energy from the wood and water elements, bringing life-enhancing chi into your sleeping space.

Incense sticks symbolize the fire element, and their smoke burns away harmful chi.

# Activating creativity in work areas 67

Make a conscious effort to stimulate creative chi in the work areas of your home, especially if you work from a home office. In this case take advantage of the fact that the arrangement and décor of your office is entirely under your control.

Most importantly your work space must benefit from plenty of yang energy, which stimulates your vitality as well as your creativity. Yang energy requires the office to be well lit and have the benefit of natural sounds such as the rustling of leaves or the flow of water from a miniature water feature.

## Benefiting from primary colours

A burst of energizing colour activates the space, and may come from a flower arrangement, a piece of art or a well-chosen shade of paint on the walls. A good dose of primary colours is excellent as these have not been diluted with other shades and are entirely yang in energy. Avoid sombre colours in your home work area as they are likely to dull your energy.

While it is good to include features that stimulate your senses, keep a balance. For this it is helpful to try to include objects that represent all five elements in the overall décor of the room. Once your work area is full of positive chi, you are certain to be rewarded with a great many new and creative ideas.

Yang energy must be activated, so your work space should be airy and well lit. Keep clutter to a minimum.

# 68 Ensuring mental clarity in study areas

*A table with a smooth, flat surface forms an ideal work space. Plenty of daylight will enhance the area with stimulating yang energy.*

Children who have started at school, as well as teenagers attending college, need a corner where they can study effectively. Ideally, this corner will enable them to study facing their best self-development direction – known as the Fu Wei direction. This enhances their concentration and enables them to develop mental clarity.

To work out the correct direction for your child to face in, you need to calculate his or her personal Kua number (see the table below), which is based on the lunar year of birth. This determines which of the eight primary and secondary directions brings concentration during study and the best exam luck.

## ENERGY TIP

### Finding out your child's Kua number

To determine the Kua number of your child, select the lunar year of birth. This is the same as the western year except for those born in January 1 or February 4. For such people, deduct 1 from the sum of the last two digits of their year of birth. For example, someone born in 1948 would add 4 + 8 to get 12, then 1+2 to get 3. (If that person were born before the lunar new year, however, deduct 1 to get 2.) If the child is male, deduct that number from 10 and, if the child is female, add it to 5.

So for male children the Kua number is 10-3 =7
For female children the Kua number is 5+3 = 8

Now look at the table below, which gives the best direction to face while doing schoolwork or studying for examinations.

| KUA | 1 | 2 | 3 | 4 | 5 | 6 | 7 | 8 | 9 |
|---|---|---|---|---|---|---|---|---|---|
| Best direction | north | SW | east | SE | * | NW | west | NE | south |

\* If the child is male, the direction is southwest and if female the direction is northeast.

## The right desk helps bring success

To enhance your child's study area, it also helps to choose a suitable desk or table. Its surface should be level, and there should be nothing about it that your child finds disconcerting or awkward. Seek your child's opinion on this. For example, do not choose a desk that has an overhanging set of drawers or cupboard. The best work desk is larger than the normal standard-size desk seen at school. In fact the larger the desk the better, as this increases your child's success.

To stimulate mental clarity place a quartz crystal, with a single point, on the desk. Encourage your child not to let the crystal absorb other people's energy. He or she should place it on the desk while studying and carry it into the examination hall as a good luck charm.

## Chapter Four

# Tapping into Your Inner Spiritual Power

Work at creating channels for the inner spirituality within you to flow outwards. This will add to your charisma, make you a lot more attractive and definitely give your words enhanced power. These are the things that bring you success and happiness. Moreover, the special energy unleashed will dispel all negatives such as depression, selfishness, anger and intolerance.

Whether you are living in a penthouse in New York or a hut in the Himalayan mountains, you will be activating the same power that lies within us all – the power that helps us work with the energy of time and space. Going spiritual does not require you to be anything other than what you are. Do not set unrealistic goals or imprison yourself behind man-made taboos. Empowering your mind should be a liberating experience, not a stifling one. All it calls for is an internalized purity of good motivation... not any outward show of 'holiness'. When you use your mind this way you will maximize your potential for success a thousandfold.

# 69 Engage your inner spiritual power and tune in mentally

As all knowledge, all experiences and all our life's outcomes emanate from the mind, the most effective practitioners of feng shui are not necessarily the most learned or the oldest, they are the most experienced and the humblest and they recognize and use the power of their own minds.

I have discovered over many years of observation that the most effective feng shui masters are no different from successful professionals in other fields of endeavour – they are always the ones who are the most relaxed and the most humble – but they also possess a quiet and reassuring steely confidence that seems to come from deep within them.

These were the Taoist masters I was most fortunate to meet and closely observe doing their work. They were not necessarily particularly famous but amongst a private circle of feng shui masters they were highly respected.

## Spiritual clarity

These Taoist feng shui masters of Hong Kong were deeply spiritual, although when you first met them you might not have thought so. They were master meditators whose minds were powerful and clear. They were always relaxed and always good-humoured, and when they made recommendations to clients, it would be obvious that they could accurately see the end result of their recommendation in their mind. They described what had to be done as though it were a picture that they could see with absolute clarity.

In the process they seemed to be imbuing their advice with an inner spiritual power, which later I was to discover we can all harness in the same way.

## Delve into your mind

The secret lies in going deep into your mind and engaging your spiritual potential to add a kind of divine strength to your actions. The magic 'open sesame' lies in the purity of your motivation: when feng shui is practised with genuine good intentions to benefit the people living within a home, it takes on great power. This chapter is devoted to introducing the ideas of delving far into your subconscious.

Start by learning how to delve into the depths of your own consciousness with simple meditation exercises that let the chi flow into your body.

---

### ENERGY TIP

## Meditate daily to gain inner awareness

Close your eyes to shut out distractions, breathe normally, stay relaxed and then direct your mind to go deep inside yourself.

Do this for a few moments each day until you become familiar with the exercise. It will soon help you rest your mind and make it clearer, opening the inner depths of your mind, your own thought processes to you.

# Spiritual means the mind – try to understand its potential  70

The word 'spiritual' refers to the mind, and spiritual people are those who seek to maximize the mind's potential. When you understand that it is your mind that has ultimate control over everything that happens to you, your chi and your space, you will come to understand the far-reaching consequences of your belief systems, your attitudes, behaviour, actions, speech and responses. Both singly and collectively these have an effect on the outcome of all your actions. But the space you live in and the chi that surrounds you also influence your life, so your mind must be harnessed to enhance the arrangement and design of your surroundings.

## The power of yin

This practice of inner feng shui is also referred to as 'the power of yin – the silent inner reaches of the mind'. Yin – as in yin and yang – always features strongly when one taps into the potential of the inner divine self, which is, of course, simply another way of describing the mind.

When your mind is positive everything you do to improve the feng shui of your space will be strengthened and made a thousand times more effective. When you add on the empowering strength of your mind, the effects get magnified even more.

Thus something as simple as placing a symbolic object in a certain corner of your home is sure to take on greater power to bring you new success when accompanied with a powerful inner intention, helping empower something that is already cosmically correct. Imagine how powerful that can be!

Calm your mind by inviting a holy object such as this Buddha figure into your home. The best place for such a statue is in the northwest of any room.

## Rise above your own negativities

When you begin to really believe in the power of your mind to enhance your practice of feng shui, any lingering depression is spontaneously dispelled. Failure becomes a thing of the past and all afflictions caused by outer cosmic forces can be overcome.

When you know you can rise above the negativities of the environment around you, and that there are simply no limits to your power over intangible afflictions, you have started practising inner feng shui. This added dimension of your use of feng shui is certain to magnify the potency of the ancient practice of space enhancement a thousandfold.

# 71 Unlock inner wisdom with pure motivation

Through meditation we can all benefit from harnessing our inner chi.

Unlocking the inner wisdom within us has less to do with formulas and methods and more to do with instinct and the spiritual connections that our minds make with the cosmic forces. Our own inner chi is not as powerful as the universal cosmic chi, but when we know how to access it, we can begin to work at synchronizing it with cosmic chi.

Good feng shui has always been about living in harmony with our world – and when we practise inner feng shui we are energizing our world by using the inner chi within to be in sync with the cosmic chi.

### Accessing our inner chi

The purity and enormous power of your mind is only fully attainable when our motives are positive.

According to the Taoist masters, to gain mastery of our inner chi requires practice over many lifetimes. It is something that is totally spiritual, requiring years of meditative practice and a renunciation of negativities. The good news is that we do not need to become master

yogics to be able to access inner chi. As long as our goals stay simple and we establish the correct motivation for becoming spiritual, we will succeed in achieving a small measure of success in opening up some of the mind's enormous power and potential. The key here is motivation: it must be pure and devoid of hidden negative agendas. A pure motivation is one that is altruistic and giving. Inner spirituality has no power when fuelled by negative anger, jealousy or greed.

The key to using mental power is to be able to establish and maintain this purity, so always check your motives before you begin. When you practise inner feng shui with the thought of benefiting others – your family, your children, your friends, your clients – it takes on a life of its own, imbuing your practice with a special power that guarantees progress.

# Undertake mental spring-cleaning  72

You must next rid your mind and thought processes of negative intentions. Getting rich, attaining success or a good name, attracting love and so forth can either be fuelled by positive or negative motivations. Positive aspirations aim to make yourself and others into happier people. As long as you are not using your feng shui knowledge to harm others, your intention is pure.

So if any cobwebs and negativities inside your mind blur your vision of the true nature of your motives, you must sweep them away. Your mind is like a mirror: when it is clear, the images reflected are sharp and lucid but when the mind is cluttered with delusions, negativities and hang-ups accumulated over a lifetime, the reflected images are blurred, unfocused and misleading.

To access the power of the mind to strengthen the effectiveness of your feng shui practice, you should therefore regularly undertake what can be described as a mental spring-cleaning of your attitudes and your aspirations. This will sweep away the dirt that clouds your visions, removing all lingering negativities.

Sweep away your negative thought patterns and aspire to mental clarity.

# Taking control of your attitudes  73

A meaningful side effect of accessing the mind and delving deep into your inner chi is that it gives you a broader vision of the world. It enhances your perceptions, showing the attitudes you adopt in greater perspective and bringing your aspirations in tune with those of others, guiding your chi to greater affinity with the chi around you.

This is what living in harmony with the environment really means. In becoming aware of your attitudes and taking control over them, you will develop a much better command of your circumstances and the outcomes of your efforts and endeavours. This is intrinsic to the overall philosophy of feng shui, seeing ourselves and our existence in relation to the things around us – our homes, our spaces, the objects we live with, the directions we align our energies with and the five elements that interact with our being.

### Heaven, earth and mankind

Taoism describes this as the concept of the whole. In feng shui we describe it as the trinity of heaven, earth and mankind. When we live in a state of this trinity, or 'tien ti ren', we are blessed with excellent energy and excellent feng shui. It is impossible to gain mastery over all the components of this concept, but with time, the practice will become second nature.

# 74 Using yin and yang, left and right brains

The effective feng shui practitioner is the one who works through both the left and right sides of the brain to engage the yin and yang of their mind.

The left side of the brain handles numbers, sequences, logic, organization and other matters requiring rational thought, reasoning, deductive and analytical considerations. Left-brain thinkers are more at home with things mathematical and scientific, focusing on lines and formulae, ignoring the subtleties of colour and cadence. They are more systematic in their approach, more detached and less emotional.

Right-brain people tend to trust themselves and their feelings more, encouraging their sixth sense to rise. The right brain handles dreaming, colours, rhythms, and the more instinctive thought processes requiring creativity, imagination, originality, inventiveness and artistic flair. Right-brain thinking is less restrained, less bounded by scientific parameters, focusing on forms and shapes, hues and subtleties, while overlooking measurements and dimensions.

*Try to combine the analytical left side and imaginative right side of your brain, emulating the beauty and scholarship of Leonardo da Vinci.*

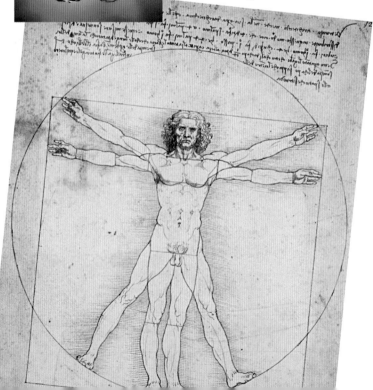

## Be both rational and instinctive

In feng shui you must use both your left and right brains, enabling you to marry the cold yin rationale of technique and formula with the warm yang comfort of your instincts.

If you only think logically, excluding creativity, your feng shui practice will have limited effectiveness. You must apply feng shui principles outside rigidly set boundaries and not become one dimensional in your practice.

Similarly, those who only use their instincts without studying the methods are sure to be tremendously handicapped. They will find their attempts are hopelessly inadequate without the rationale within which the science of feng shui is practised.

The best results come to those who activate both their creative and rational brains. The effect of actively engaging two brains working together is far more effective than when one side of the brain is functioning to the exclusion of the other.

Two brains working simultaneously produce better results, so be neither too believing nor too disbelieving. Be rational, but also trust your instincts. This really demonstrates the wisdom of the tai chi because the left and right sides of the brain are the yin and yang of our brain!

# Getting rid of imagined limits  75

Those who have ever attended a lecture on positive thinking will know about setting limits. Most of the time we create breaks and hindrances to our own potential by marking out the limits of our own capabilities. This does not refer only to our perception of ability, it also encompasses the sense of worthiness. Many people simply do not believe they deserve a better life, or that they can be happier, or that they can aspire to have a better lifestyle.

## Think big

Most of the time, our success is blocked by our own view of our world. In your efforts to increase your potential and enhance the results of your feng shui, do not be afraid to think big, or have big dreams. You must shrug off imagined limits to your own capabilities.

## Remove the barriers to success

Systematically dissolve all the blockages in your mind and supplement this exercise by also removing any physical blockages in your home to let the energy flow unencumbered around your home. Let the invisible energies flow freely without breaks and just as mental limits benefit from a breath of fresh air, likewise the energy of your home also benefits, so leave at least a couple of windows open and if possible keep some of your doors open as well. Let the outdoors come inside… unblock the blockages and you will be removing limitations from your life.

Opening doors allows chi to flow unhindered through the rooms of your home.

### ENERGY TIP

## Let chi flow through your home

Ensure that the chi can flow easily through your home by removing any awkward furniture arrangements and opening up tight corners. Open your windows to let the energy enter the house easily.

# 76 Thinking rich – discard poverty programming

Once you are used to actively engaging your mind in your feng shui practice you should simultaneously engage in prosperity programming. Live your life as though you are rich and wealthy. Fill your dining tables with plenty of food, signifying abundance; always serve more than you need, especially when you have guests, and invite lots of people (who should then be well disposed towards you) to come to your home. Having people eat as your guests creates prosperity programming and strengthens the yang energy of your home.

*Ensuring there is a plentiful quantity of food available to your family and friends will help programme you against poverty.*

*A generous dining table symbolizes the wealth that you are trying to attain.*

## Don't worry, live to the full

You must also guard strongly against poverty programming – don't always worry about a rainy day. People who are generous are programming themselves for a life of prosperity, while those people who are miserly towards others are actually programming themselves for poverty.

Don't let the simple things such as saving money on electricity by turning off the lights or closing the windows because you think it might rain take over your life. The more relaxed you are about money

and everything that is connected with spending, the more likely you are to make your finances grow.

## Generosity builds wealth

Feng shui to attract wealth rarely works well for stingy people with closed minds. It works beautifully for people who are expansive and generous. So adjust your attitudes as well as your motivations.

# Neutralizing your inner adversaries – developing the art of yielding  77

The biggest hindrance to success – whether at work, in the home or in our relationships – lies within ourselves. The most dangerous enemy in our quest to achieve a happier, healthier and more vital lifestyle is the adversary within us. It casts doubt on our worthiness to create a good lifestyle for ourselves and causes whatever is done to enhance harmony and balance in our space to get out of sync, making the changes less effective.

**Relax, relax, relax**

The secret of making effective feng shui changes to your home is to do so with a relaxed mindset. Never allow your mind to cause you to doubt yourself. Be as relaxed as you can when you try to implement some of the suggestions in this book and neutralize your inner doubts with an attitude of strength and confidence. Often when some feng shui change is not done correctly, it shows up pretty fast and then all that is needed is some adjustment. So try never to lose confidence in your own feng shui practice.

Create a happy, calm lifestyle to enhance harmony and make the most of the feng shui changes you make.

# Visualize and actualize – accessing your inner subconscious  78

Borrow the powerful techniques of actualization through visualization from the Siddhi yogics and Taoist masters. Indeed, the use of powerful mental visualizations to bring power and success to our intentions and wishes lies in using the mind to create pictures that have a canny way of becoming reality. So when you arrange your living space, move furniture around, align sitting and sleeping directions to your own personal good directions and place symbolic cures or enhancers in different corners of rooms, make sure that you accompany your actions with strong visualizations of success.

At first it will not be easy since effective visualization requires practice, and those that lead to success require imagination as well. Think of all the outcomes you are wishing for as you feng shui the rooms of your home. It is this visualization that will cause you to actualize all wishes into reality.

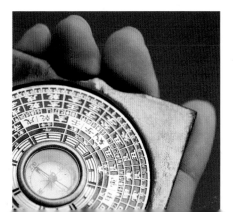

Use a compass to help align your interiors to match your own personal good directions.

# 79 Clearing inner channels of energy

During visualization you should make a special effort to clear the energy channels within your physical body. These cause hindrances to success just like mental blockages: the Chinese always refer to the inner chi of our beings as being even more powerful than our external chi. So it is advisable to get rid of the mental clutter that has a way of regurgitating itself and blocking your channels of energy.

Spend ten minutes each day mentally going through the rooms of your house in which you live and spend time. Meditate on your space and imagine a gust of fresh air sweeping away the cobwebs and the clutter that tends to stick in the mind after a hard day's work. And here's a tip: try to create a situation in which you actually feel a gush of fresh cold air, so that you can recreate its refreshing feeling in your mind. This is such a powerful technique that making it a part of your inner feng shui practice should be high on your list of priorities.

# 80 Nurture the spiritual essence of mankind luck

Good feng shui is about creating the presence of tien ti ren, the 'heaven, earth and mankind' trinity of energies in the home. The last two are within our control and of these it is mankind energy that determines whether one enjoys good luck or bad.

## Dispel depression and worry

We all exude mankind energy so we should consciously exude good chi. When we are angry and depressed, or worry all the time, the energy created can be harmfully negative.

This has a tendency to worsen as the mind dwells on negatives. So as soon as you start reading this book, make a real effort to suppress any tendency to stay attached to your depressive state of mind and shrug off these feelings. If you want good feng shui in your home, try to shake off negative expectations.

Instead, become an Empress of optimism. Expect good things to happen and you will be surprised to discover that they always do. This way you are nurturing your inner spirit and inner essence.

# Secrets of powerful sleeping  81

To bring out the best of the personal chi energies within the human body, it is beneficial, even necessary, to develop power sleeping, what the masters refer to as the 'yoga of sleeping'. This involves sleeping at the most beneficial times, and also in the correct way.

The best time to go to bed each evening is around 11 pm. In any case you should always make sure you are in bed and the lights are turned off by 11 pm. This is the ideal because cell rejuvenation in the body is reported to take place at the first hour of the Zodiac, i.e. during the Hour of the Rat, which is between 11 pm and 1 am. If the body is not in a state of sleep the cells cannot rejuvenate, allowing the chi to become weakened. Over time when the energy has not had the chance to get replenished or rejuvenated energy becomes stagnated, making it difficult, and eventually impossible, for the person to benefit from good surroundings. The feng shui of your home cannot help you when you are in a weakened chi state. When chi energy is not replenished, the constitution of the body loses vigour and vitality.

## The power of sleep

Sleeping by 11 pm also ensures enough hours of sleep. This is something that Western medical science and Ayurvedic sciences also encourage. Only then can you access your deep sleep level. And to ensure that you get the best feng shui while you sleep, also make very certain that you sleep with your head pointed to your most auspicious direction, based on the Eight Mansions feng shui formula of personalized best directions.

Be in bed by 11 pm every night to ensure you are asleep by the first hour of the Zodiac, allowing your body the best chance of cell rejuvenation.

# 82 Yoga dreaming turns happy dreams into reality

Place the Eight Immortals, here represented by these coins, near your bed to encourage auspicious dreams.

The Maha Siddhis found in many Eastern cultures are acknowledged as holy men who have realized the highest powers of yoga. Through their immense knowledge they teach the ability to move eventually from the yoga of sleeping to the yoga of dreaming. This is achieved by developing healthy disciplines for resting the body and rejuvenating the mind.

Your body will benefit from a set routine of good habits. By adopting such a routine you allow your body's energy to interact harmoniously with the energy of your surroundings. This makes it possible for you to start developing the art of yoga dreaming.

## Achieving spiritual clarity

Yoga dreaming is a way of training your conscious mind to sleep while your subconscious, dreaming mind stays awake and alert to mindful meditations. You can use this kind of dreaming to bring good luck into your life,

perhaps inducing an auspicious turn of events. Pleasant dreams always lead to happy outcomes, so yoga dreaming allows an auspicious inner world to enhance every aspect of your life.

## Creating auspicious dreams

To assist you in creating your personal auspicious dreams, place a symbol of the Eight Immortals near your bed and kushi grass under your pillow. The Eight Immortals are Chinese deities charged with helping people achieve their goals and bestowing happiness, health and good fortune.

## ENERGY TIP

### Stimulating the mind to dream

Encourage your subconscious mind to dream, and to retain the memories of your dreams, by placing kushi grass underneath your pillow. Over time your dreams will become more and more auspicious. Dreams of pleasant places, life enhancing events and fulfilling relationships will gradually become your reality.

# Activating creativity and innovation  83

Crystals are stimulating for your mind, enhancing your creativity. Placing suitable crystals underneath your bed inspires your subconscious with innovative thoughts that will benefit your life.

## Quartz crystals for yang energy

Choose pointed quartz crystals. They need not be large but it helps if they have been properly cleansed with rock or sea salt. Use three crystals to start with, and arrange them under your bed to form an arrow shape directly below your head. Not everyone can cope with the heightened yang energy sent out by the crystals, so allow yourself time to adjust. Crystals emit a power not many people are familiar with, and it will take time for your body's chi to become accustomed to it. However, your creativity will soon receive a boost of positive energy.

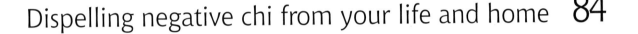

Siting pointed crystals cleansed with salt underneath your bed will help develop innovative thought.

# Dispelling negative chi from your life and home  84

Anger, jealousy and other strong negative feelings are amongst the greatest cause of bad feng shui. It is beneficial to dissolve such harmful energy from your mind and body if you are to re-energize your living space effectively. Unhappiness in the air is the greatest killer of good feng shui.

## Creating space for positive chi

Negative thoughts or worries can be habit-forming. Notice if you tend to dwell on problems and make a positive effort to take action to resolve situations rather than fret about them. Consider the people who arouse your negative emotions, and try to minimize their roles in your life. If you are self-critical, be kinder to yourself.

In this way you are consciously dispelling the bad chi afflicting you. This also creates space for good chi to enter your life as negativity evaporates from the cosmic chi that surrounds you. A happy home almost always enjoys good feng shui.

Happy family relationships ensure bad chi is kept at bay.

## 85 Creating mental magic

Your mind has the power to create your reality. Legends in which magic features almost always involve the deep, inner concentration of gifted, spiritual people. The key to unlocking your own mental magic lies in your ability to focus your mind on a goal and to visualise yourself achieving that goal.

### Power of visualizations

Relaxing your mind and body so as to concentrate strongly on a particular thought is a skill that only comes with practice. It means cultivating an active, vigorous mind and not allowing yourself to become lazy. Set aside a little time each day to exercise your mind in the same way as you set aside time to exercise your body.

Creating pictures, or visualisations, and focusing your mind on them, is a powerful way to influence your outer reality. Visualise successful scenarios for yourself and your family, and combine these mental exercises with good physical feng shui in the arrangement of your home. You will soon find that you achieve success in all areas of your life – including career, prosperity and relationships – faster than before and with greater ease.

## 86 Symbols manifest powerful realities

Since the beginning of time the Universe has hidden its magic in codes – numbers, shapes, colours and dimensions. These contain powerful truths and auspicious signs that are only revealed through the many symbols that surround us. Many people are unaware of the significance of these symbols, but they have always been the key to unlocking the secrets of the Cosmos.

### Feng shui truths

Understanding feng shui's many different formulas is dependent on symbols. They make it possible to decipher the hidden codes of the Pa Kua and the Lo Shu square. Of all the symbols in feng shui, it is the broken and unbroken lines of trigram combinations that reveal the greatest treasures of feng shui knowledge.

### Spiritual clarity

At its most basic level, feng shui practice involves the best placement of symbols of good fortune and protection within the home and office to enhance spaces with beneficial chi. Placing lucky objects inside the home, based on the different 'formulas' of feng shui, is a powerful way to re-energize previously stagnant space.

A space empty of auspicious decorative objects will likewise be devoid of positive chi. By inviting objects symbolic of good fortune into your home, you introduce the positive benefits of good feng shui.

The eight trigrams incorporated in the Pa Kua are the most commonly used symbols that help reveal feng shui knowledge.

# Tap the power within you – daily practice   87

To activate your good luck regularly, develop the habit of practising mental feng shui daily . Walk through the rooms of your home and around your garden. Think about what you would like to change, replace or improve.

Develop a deep familiarity with the rooms of your home. This daily exercise in awareness does not take long but helps to stimulate new ideas that will allow you to enhance your home's energy.

Not many people picture their houses accurately, and are often unable to recollect every nook and cranny. Developing a habit of awareness of the space you live in is essential to improving its good fortune energy.

## New awareness brings change

By increasing your awareness of your home, you are enhancing it with the vital essence of your own energy. In just a week of carrying out the daily exercise, you will see what I mean. Let your inner power guide you and, within a few months, you will have changed the appearance, the feel and the mood of all your rooms. The changes you introduce will probably be so gradual that you will be unconscious of the full effect of the transformation.

Walk around your home every day, letting your instincts guide you to make changes.

## 88 Supplement your feng shui with positive expectations

Take time to focus your mind on the happiness of waking up to a new day.

You will also benefit from writing down your positive expectations.

In all the years I have practised feng shui, I have always simultaneously applied the power of positive expectations to my life. I consciously create graphic novels inside my head which star myself, always happy and smiling, and laughing with my family and close friends. In making it a life-long habit to dream of happy outcomes, I believe I have brought myself much good fortune.

### Wake up to happiness

You, too, can enhance your feng shui practice with the visualisation exercise that only good news comes to you, only good people enter your life and only good results come from all your actions.

To help you get started here is a morning mental exercise that you can introduce easily into your daily life. Always allow a little time in the morning for lying in a half-asleep mode simply focussing your mind on the happiness of waking up to a brand new day, alive and well. Focus on the positive outcomes you would like to achieve today. Whatever it is you expect of the day, make a conscious wish for it to be free of aggravations, bad news and bad incidents. Concentrate on feeling positive about what is in store for you.

# White light meditation – cocooning your home    89

Protection is a vital part of feng shui, safe-guarding you and your family from misfortune, accidents and tragedies. In protective feng shui, your inner spirituality and ability to live in a state of awareness is especially powerful. A protective visualization for you or a member of your family might be of a shield or armour warding off negative, harmful energy.

## Focussing your mental powers

One of the best protective visualizations for your home – and thereby you and your family – is to create a white light that cocoons your entire house and garden. This protective visualization is usually referred to as white light meditation. The protective cocoon of cosmic energy has great power.

## Activating cosmic energy

Create the mental picture of white light embracing your home each night just before going to sleep. You are creating protection for everyone living in your home during the night-time yin hours.

If you make this visualization part of your night-time routine, you will strengthen your mind's ability to focus. Soon it will take you less than a minute before sleeping to create your protective visual force field. You are directing cosmic energy to surround your home and keep everyone safe while they sleep.

Protect yourself and your home from nighttime yin energy by practising white light meditation.

# Chapter Five

# Creating Powerful Personal Charisma

This section is devoted to enhancing your physical and spiritual health, and I will share with you feng shui secrets for good looks and a strong body. Attention to personal grooming is as important in attracting good fortune as how you arrange your home. Simply by wearing auspicious colours you can attract lucky chi. If you exude yang energy, other people will find you charismatic and you will attract relationship luck as well as success in your career.

There are also feng shui practices to strengthen your aura and imbue you with a magnetism that attracts happiness and easy success. There are empowering benefits to treating your body spiritually. Enhancing your practice this way will open pathways into the mind's inner recesses, which in turn leads to better potency and, if you are lucky, also the awakening and rise of genuine wisdom.

# An auspicious face reflects inner vibrancy 90

No face, no matter how beautiful or well balanced the features, can be charismatic or auspicious if it does not reflect the vibrant personality within. Charisma is not about having perfect features, a fine complexion or a good figure. It is not the packaging that creates charisma, but the projection of the personality. If your personality radiates yang chi then your aura will give you a presence in any room that will attract people to you.

## Developing charisma

To bring out your powerful personal charisma, start by creating brightness and lightness within yourself. You must think powerful to become powerful, and love the uniqueness of your own appearance to be beautiful. Perhaps most important of all, believe that your whole personality has a resounding vibrancy that gives you a presence.

This belief in yourself does not come overnight, but is built up over time. The sooner you make a start, the sooner your inner charisma will begin shining through. Often the inner vibrancy you are seeking to develop is enhanced by the belief that you look good. In this way there is a simultaneous boost to the radiancy of your inner self and outer self. The more one is enhanced, the more the other benefits, and vice versa.

Taking care of your appearance encourages a sense of wellbeing from which charisma can grow.

ENERGY TIP

### Begin creating an auspicious face by always looking your best

Paying attention to your physical wellbeing and personal grooming is an ideal way to start creating your auspicious face. The very act of making an extra effort with your physical appearance, perhaps using make-up to give you a healthy glow, will give your confidence the kind of boost that jump-starts personal charisma.

# 91 Harmony of yin and yang attracts good chi

Aim to create a good balance in your life, as this will give you inner tranquillity.

Nothing is as beneficial as having a good balance of yin and yang chi in your physical body and appearance. As well as ensuring good health, this harmonious combination of female and male chi – representing the wholeness of the 'Tai Chi' – is what creates the inner serenity that others find attractive.

## Harmonize your body and mind

Harmonizing yin and yang in your life often means striking a good balance in all the things you do, as well as in your surroundings. Think of opposite characteristics: softness and toughness, coolness and warmth, quiet and noise, dark and light. Keeping a balance is not as difficult as it sounds. All that is needed is a conscious effort not to go to any extreme in the way you live. Good feng shui living encourages moderation in everything you do.

## Find life's rhythm

When your body is not excessively taxed in any way, it is able to rejuvenate itself. Similarly, do not allow your mental powers to become exhausted by making too many demands of

The ancient symbol of yin and yang clearly represents two opposites working together while remaining individual.

yourself – or allowing others to do so. The same is true of your emotional energy. Make sure your daily timetable includes appropriate amounts of rest time and work time without too much of either.

With this kind of harmony, you will never feel too tired or aggravated. Your life will flow at a pace that creates a relaxed inner calmness that others will find restful and attractive.

# Five important features of your face   92

In Chinese culture, your face is said to be a mirror to your soul. It often shows a lot more than you want to reveal about yourself, which is why masks have such an important place in Chinese tradition. Indeed, in old China, officials at court learned early on to hide their feelings, their moods and their attitudes. They consciously worked on not allowing what was in their hearts and souls to show on their faces. Many of the secrets of the 'hidden face' are now lost, although references to them continue to colour the metaphors of local dialects of the Chinese language.

## Mystery creates charisma

Today, we use cosmetics to define our features, drawing attention to our eyes and mouths. We use foundation cream to make our skins look as flawless as possible, evening out our complexions. Making up our faces is the modern equivalent of creating a mask – though the effects are more subtle.

Let your face look groomed and beautiful. If you choose to use cosmetics to improve your

**ENERGY TIP**
## What gives your appearance personality?

The forehead, cheeks, eyes, nose and mouth are the five most important defining features that give flesh and substance to your overall appearance.

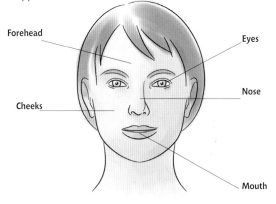

Forehead · Eyes · Nose · Cheeks · Mouth

appearance, you can look on make-up as a mask that conceals your inner self, or as a way to emphasize the best in you. For example, a colourful shade of lipstick enhances the positive effect of a smiling or laughing mouth.

Remember that you are in control of the persona you are creating. Make up is the first step towards projecting your personality while not revealing everything about yourself. Mystery is a vital ingredient of charisma.

## Know your own face

Just as it is important to develop an awareness of the rooms in your home, it is beneficial to know your own face well. This is not as easy as it sounds – other people see your different expressions but you only see yourself reflected in a mirror. However, make the effort to discover the colours that suit you and how to enhance your features.

Chinese masks focus on the five features that give vibrancy to a face.

# 93    Keep cheeks flushed to exude yang energy

To make yourself look more attractive, and to enhance your relationship luck, make good use of cosmetic blushers that rouge the cheeks. I cannot begin to tell you how auspicious it is to bring colour to your cheeks, especially if you are a woman. Blush-tinted cheeks make you look healthy and imbue your whole face with yang energy, attracting people to you.

Single women will especially benefit from wearing some colour on their cheeks, as their glowing looks will draw more suitors. When your cheeks are colourless, you run the danger of creating the impression of a sallow, dull, pallid and unexciting person. All these negatives are removed the minute you put some colour on your cheeks, transforming your face instantly.

## My personal secret of success

Do not allow anyone to dissuade you from following this advice. In my early career days when I used to go to work and attend company functions with plenty of rouge colour on my cheeks jealous colleagues used to refer to me cattily as the 'opera star'… but when I was promoted every three months and those same people came to work under me, the talking stopped. I never told them the secret of my success.

These days I still wear colour on my cheeks but not all the time. I have had more than enough success luck and I need a break. But for every special occasion, every important meeting and every vital encounter I still wear blusher with abandon! You should too – you'll be surprised to see how the yang energy lights up your face when you do.

Always colour your cheeks with rouge to enhance both relationship and career luck.

# Spotlight one dominant colour  94

When you dress and make up your face, always focus on one dominant colour. This might reflect either an auspicious element based on your best Kua compass directions or the element of the day. To find out your Kua number and best compass directions, or to check the element of the day, visit www.wofs.com. Also on this site you will find the feng shui almanac, which tells you if the day is auspicious for you.

## Wearing auspicious colours

When the day is auspicious, enhance the element of the day and, when it is inauspicious, exhaust the element of that day. Take note that red is fire, yellow is earth, green is wood, black and blue are water, white and metallic are metal. So, for example, if the day is auspicious for you and its element is fire, wear red for good fortune. If the day is inauspicious wear blue or black to deflect bad luck.

## Combining colours

There are also some particularly auspicious colour combinations, which are shown in the table on the right. All these are excellent. They create a positive harmony that will attract lucky chi towards you.

You can vary the shades of the colours in the table as you wish – for example, you might want to combine a golden yellow with a russet red. The combinations will enhance your yang chi, attracting people to you and creating success in all areas of your life.

The Pa Kua formula is a helpful means of finding out how to attract lucky chi and avoid unlucky chi. If you know your Kua number, you can discover your most auspicious compass directions and your unlucky directions.

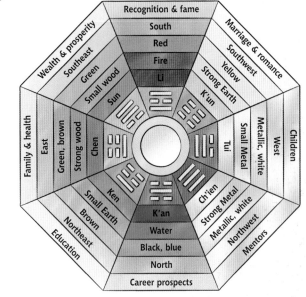

## Auspicious colour combinations:

- Blue or black with green
- Brown and red
- Red and yellow
- Yellow and white
- White and black

# 95 A well shaped nose creates a 'mountain of success' for prosperity luck

In feng shui, the part of the face that determines prosperity luck is the nose. The Chinese revere people with high noses. This is especially true when such noses are not thin, which can give the face a starved look. If a high nose is well shaped it creates what is referred to as 'mountains of success in our middle zone'.

## Considering your nose shape

In Chinese face reading a straight nose is considered to be preferable, particularly so if it does not tilt upwards or downwards too noticeably at the tip. Although it is best for a nose not to be thin, equally it should not appear too fleshy.

If your nose is well shaped it creates what is known as a "mountain" on your face that will bring you plenty of success luck. Because your nose is located in the centre of your face, whatever is central affects everything around it. So when the centre is auspicious, the rest of the body follows suit.

Whatever the shape of your nose you can enhance the way it looks with the right hairstyle, and give it a flawless appearance with cosmetics such as foundation cream.

## Discover your nose type

There are many different types of nose. Check which is nearest to yours and see how you can enhance it for best prosperity luck.

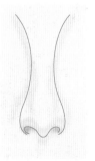

**Thin nose:**
Use cosmetics such as bronzer to make a thin nose look more shapely.

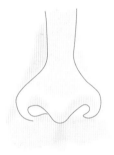

**Fleshy nose:**
Too prominent a nose can also detract from prosperity luck.

**Rounded nose:**
Use cosmetics to reduce the appearance of fleshiness, perhaps shading the sides.

**High nose:**
Sitting high on the face is an auspicious sign.

**Straight nose:**
A straight, strong nose creates a 'mountain of success'.

# A clear complexion attracts harmony and luck   96

rough, so it is a good idea to reduce the direct impact of sunlight. Wear a large, shading sun hat and a sun cream to protect your face from damaging ultra-violet rays. Some sunlight, however, is vital for invigorating yang energy – think of the uplifting effect of looking at the first rays of sunlight in the morning.

Your face benefits from Moon energy. This is echoed by pearlescent powders, which add sheen and clarity to your face. The Chinese prefer the face to resemble the Moon rather than the Sun, hence the preference for pale rather than suntanned faces.

A pale face reflects moonlight, which is auspicious and preferable to a tanned face.

The first step to a flawless complexion is to keep your skin clean and well moisturized.

According to the Chinese a smooth complexion is the most important ingredient of a lucky face. So today's breakthroughs in facial creams are a real boon for those wanting to create a charismatic and successful face. Always make sure you clean your face regularly each night before going to bed.

## Mixing yin and yang

The secret to an auspicious face is the right mix of yin and yang chi. Too much yang sunlight causes the face to crease and become

# 97 Bright eyes and a steady gaze brings good chi

Your eyes reveal so much about you: your health, your mood, your character and your emotions. They are the windows to what is in your heart. People discover so much about you just by looking into your eyes. Every morning, as you prepare for the day, pay attention to how your eyes will appear to others. If you want to create an impression of vitality and intelligence, it is vital that your eyes sparkle.

## Inauspicious tired eyes

Tired, dry or red eyes reflect a listlessness or instability of energy within our minds and bodies. Often they are the first indications of excessive 'heat' in the body. Whatever the cause, tired eyes are never auspicious, so there is no need even to mention bloodshot eyes! Tired eyes have a dullness to them that is very uninspiring. They are usually an indication that you need plenty of sleep or some restful yin chi. If you make a conscious effort to light up your eyes, treating them for redness or dryness, and making sure that you get enough sleep, they will enhance your personal charisma.

## Let your eyes speak

Bright eyes are a magnet, attracting helpful people who bring plenty of good chi and wonderful opportunities. You can also use eye make-up to define your eyes and add lustre to your eyelids.

A feng shui tip is to develop the strength of your eyes so that you can keep them open without flickering. Steady eyes that have the ability to gaze straight without blinking reflect a calm personality. Some people have even developed their eye strength to make their eyes powerfully piercing, but there is no need to go that far.

Don't forget to keep a slight smile in your eyes. If you do not, you risk them looking unfriendly or, worse, hostile. Remember, good chi comes to those whose demeanour is unthreatening. Develop a steady gaze that is friendly and inviting, and meet other people's eyes in an open manner.

Project a charismatic personality by always keeping eye contact with colleagues and friends alike.

# Be well groomed every single day   98

A lucky person is always prepared to greet good fortune with a clean, well-groomed body and a happy face. My current profession as a writer requires me to work alone and at home. However, to achieve success with my writing, I make a point of bathing then putting on my make-up and jewellery every day before going into my study to sit at my computer. Even though there is normally no one else in the room while I write, I am always determined to look my best. I can also greet anyone dropping by to see me without having to rush upstairs to get ready.

## Don't become lazy

You need not be a particularly stylish or elegant person to dress well. In fact being well groomed has little to do with being stylish. However, you do need to take care of your physical appearance. Those who allow themselves to get lazy about this are usually careless people whose attitude to life will seriously detract from their mankind luck. When good fortune knocks for them, they risk not being able to recognize it.

This is why I shake my head in sadness when I see young people who delight in wearing torn and worn-out jeans when they could just as easily wear clothes

## ENERGY TIP

### Keeping yourself and your home tidy

Your clothes should always be clean and well ironed. Keep them hung or stacked neatly in your wardrobe so that they are ready when you choose to wear them. Being well groomed does not mean you need to dress formally every day but it does mean that you should make the cleanliness of both yourself and your wardrobe a personal mantra.

that are clean and in good repair. Look at all the pop stars who did this: where are they now?

## Effort breeds success

Being well groomed at all times puts you in readiness to receive good fortune when the Cosmos sends it your way. Look around at the successful people in your office or amongst the social set you mix with – you will discover it is those who make a real effort not to be sloppy or indifferent to their appearance who really enjoy meaningful success.

This is the same principle as adopting the practice of good feng shui in the home. Harmful, stagnant chi builds up from an attitude of carelessness. However, if you make an effort to keep yourself and your home clean and well cared for then the energy around you will be revitalized and fresh. You will enjoy better luck and good things will seem to happen to you all the time.

The clothes you wear should give you confidence and allow you to meet every day's unexpected challenges.

# 99

# Show your teeth as much as possible – open your mouth!

This little-known Chinese saying is often used to encourage young children to open their mouth when they smile in greeting. Showing one's teeth in a broad smile achieves many benefits. Think of the associations you might have with teeth: they are used to chew food but also to inflict a painful bite. Showing them in a flash of smile demonstrates friend-liness, warmth and lack of hostility, instantly creating good chi energy. Smiling with your mouth closed gives a less friendly message and ambience because you look less open – even appearing to hide something, perhaps your true opinion of the person you are greeting.

To make the most of your smile, brush your teeth regularly and make routine trips to the dentist and dental hygienist.

*A broad smile not only conveys warmth and happiness, it also brings good fortune by allowing in the energy of the Cosmos.*

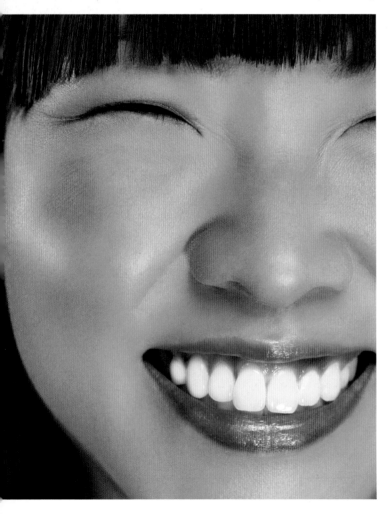

### The energy of the Cosmos

The mouth is an opening to your body. If you open your mouth frequently, you will allow the energy of the Cosmos into your being. This promotes good fortune and symbolizes always having more than enough to eat.

Traditionally, having a mole or a beauty spot near your mouth makes it even more ben-eficial to show your teeth when smiling. You will enhance your aura of goodwill and friend-liness, and attract lots of good chi back. Smiling also exercises your facial muscles, keeping your face well toned and youthful in appearance.

### Benefit from the 'power of speech'

Smiling creates good feng shui around your mouth area, ensuring that you enjoy the good fortune of successful relationships and having plenty to eat.

An open, smiling mouth also suggests that you have the gift of the gab, and are able to talk your way into and out of any situation. People who develop this ability are described as having the 'power of speech'. Often, they are charismatic, others listen to them readily and their words have impact.

# Wear jewellery every day for sparkling yang chi 100

In recent years so much attention has been focused on adding sparkle and glitter to clothes, jewellery and other accessories, and even to homes, that lots of people are benefiting from excellent yang feng shui without even being aware of it.

## Show off the 'bling'!

Adding some 'bling' to your everyday dressing is excellent feng shui. If the first thing a husband sees in the morning is his wife dressed up and wearing her jewellery, he will have good luck all day. The same is true for children. If instead of seeing their mother looking dishevelled and sleepy eyed, they see a goddess-like mother, they will also have amazing good luck.

I am not suggesting you need to get dolled up every morning, but why not add some glitter to your everyday dressing and discover the difference it makes to your day? Wear the best jewellery you can afford. Although it is very energizing to wear diamonds and other precious stones, nowadays glass gems have been so perfected that their lustre is almost like the real thing.

Both fabulous jewels and sparkling 'bling' will attract beneficial yang feng shui.

## Fabulous costume jewellery

I am bowled over by the sheer range of fun and beautiful jewellery now available. You will easily be able to find gemstone jewellery in a variety of colours that will enhance the element of the day when it is auspicious for you (see page 93). Colourful jewellery that catches the light and sparkles is a wonderful way of surrounding yourself with an aura of positive yang chi.

# 101 Activate your third eye to expand your world

Your awareness of messages received after activating the third eye will grow steadily. Focus on the imagery flashing through your brain and weave it into your consciousness.

People are now becoming familiar with the third eye, which lies just beneath the skin's surface between the eyebrows. The third eye is our mystical eye, which sees all the spiritual and psychic aspects of our worlds that our regular two eyes cannot see.

## Open your mind

To activate your third eye, focus your concentration on the area between your eyebrows. Rub this part of your face in the morning when you wake up and at night just before you go to sleep. After you have done this regularly for about a month you will start to become increasingly aware of images that flash through your mind. At first you will hardly notice them, or they will not seem significant, but over time they will weave unexpected messages and stories into your con-

The third eye lies on the forehead just beneath the surface of the skin in the centre of the face between the eyebrows.

Activate the power of the third eye by gently rubbing around it in a circular motion every morning and evening.

sciousness. By opening your third eye, you will become more aware of space and time, and this will help you slowly but surely to live a fuller and more meaningful life.

## Discover your psychic abilities

For some people rubbing the third eye also creates pathways into their inner instincts. Some people call this a psychic ability but this is not the monopoly of a chosen few – all of us have it – but sadly not many people have the confidence to trust their instincts sufficiently. When you activate your third eye, think yourself into a state of readiness for your own psychic abilities to emerge gradually.

# Keep your forehead clear and shining 102

One of the most important parts of the face is the forehead which, when clear and shining, indicates a masterful intellect and a person of great creativity and vision. When the forehead is smooth and broad it also indicates someone who will take on the sceptre of authority. It is a particularly good idea to keep your forehead clear of symbolic obstacles if you aspire to high political office or other influential position.

## Remove the hurdles

Find a hairstyle that suits you without covering your forehead. A heavy fringe is particularly inauspicious for your career and prosperity prospects, creating unnecessary hurdles to your success path. Do away with a fringe on your forehead no matter how cute it looks. Although fringes are great for young children, from a feng shui perspective they are definitely out of place on an adult face.

While a fringe is fine for a child, it is best for an adult to keep the forehead clear of hair.

A heavy fringe can mask both creativity and ambition.

Don't let your hair straggle across your face – expose your forehead.

A man's forehead is just as susceptible to the dangers of being covered by a fringe of hair.

Best of all, pull your hair away from your face to unblock your success path.

A clear forehead creates no obstacles to career success, activating prospects for advancement.

# 103 Discover your miraculous breath

If you want to develop a 'presence' – the kind of charisma that brings you attention the moment you walk into a room – make a conscious effort to develop deep breathing. The miraculous breath governs the quality of chi energy that surrounds you, so the ability to breathe strongly and steadily without any seeming effort is a powerful key to good health and an aura of positive yang chi.

## ENERGY TIP

### Practising deep breathing

Start discovering your magical breath by practising steady and deep breathing on a daily basis. Simply sit upright in a chair with your hands resting on your knees and concentrate on letting the air flow in and out of your lungs. Do this exercise until deep breathing becomes second nature, re-energizing your life and, by extension, your home.

The movements of tai chi are based around the steadiness and control of one's breathing.

## Discover extra strength and vigour

All Chinese martial arts and chi kung exercises are based on focussed breathing. This is because breathing shapes our effectiveness in all our activities. Start paying attention to your breath – most people's breathing is too shallow. At night consciously take deep breaths to sleep more soundly. When you awake, you will find that you really are more refreshed.

It is the same during your working hours. When you make a real effort to breathe more deeply something magical happens to your energy levels. Charismatic people always breathe deeply and steadily: they are rarely out of breath nor are they easily tired out.

## Positive support promotes confidence 104

Feng shui is more effective when you carry out changes with a confidence born of solid understanding and belief. The same is true of developing your personal effectiveness. Confidence in yourself makes you walk taller and face the world with greater authority.

The most confident people usually have knowledge and expertise gained through experience. It is based on a firm foundation of certainty and self-assurance.

### Surround yourself with support

To make sure that their confident attitude is maintained, self-assured people engage in a process of continuous positive programming. This means paying attention to the type of people around them.

Surround yourself with people who build you up rather than people who prick your bubble. Minimize the negative influences in your life. Do not spend your time with people who make you feel unsure of yourself, question your judgement or who constantly correct you under the guise of doing it 'for your own good'. Confidence arises from the energy you surround yourself with. When people near you are supportive your aura expands, creating confidence and success-bringing chi energy.

## When you have substance you generate 105 radiance

While it is excellent to use feng shui practise to enhance your inner and outer radiance, never forget the need to be a person of real substance. The Chinese express this ideal of all-roundedness in the trinity of heaven, earth and mankind – the three energies that are so vital to creating a harmonious, auspicious whole.

### Keep your integrity

The radiance of the self can never be enhanced if you use negative methods to magnify your aura, for instance by stealing the praise for another person's work or talking badly about others to enhance yourself. If you gossip or achieve success by pushing others down, the aura you create will be flawed. We are all by nature perfect and when we give in to base

instincts we cause flaws to appear in our auras. These are like the black holes of space and they dull our inner and outer radiance.

Authentic substance, which shines forth most strongly, always comes from hard work and genuine personal creativity, which makes you an inspiration to others.

# 106 Spiritual sounds to awaken your inner flame

Use the spiritual sounds of a recited mantra or a round of drums to add a powerful ambience to your personal space.

Enhance your personal space by awakening your inner fire with spiritual sounds. This brings a positive and divine resonance to your immediate surroundings. In the past the only way to create these special, spiritual sounds was to recite mantras, generating a rhythm to the way you chanted them. Today there are many beautifully chanted spiritual sounds available as recordings, so one is truly spoilt for choice.

Search for recordings of beautiful and powerful mantras recited in ancient monas-

teries and nunneries. By playing them in your home, you are imbuing your personal space with a special, powerful ambience.

## Flowing water for chi energy

You can enhance the ambience of your home even further with the sound of slowly flowing water in the background, which symbolizes the power of nature. The flow of water creates a chi energy that is both restful and stimulating. Being surrounded by this kind of chi strengthens your aura and brings easy success, good health and a calmness of demeanour that is very attractive to others.

The gentle chiming of metal produced by this improvised windchime creates powerful chi energy.

# Verbalize all your triumphant moments 107 – rejoice!

Give yourself permission to think and talk about times when particular aspects of your life are going well – perhaps when you achieve a goal or complete a project and feel like rejoicing. Don't be afraid to give yourself a regular pat on the back. Likewise, notice the achievements of those who are near and dear to you, and celebrate their successes with them. The power of rejoicing in all our worthwhile achievements – as well as those of other people – is a powerful catalyst to greater success in the future.

## Nurture your success

Think of each small triumph as a seed for greater success in future. Your achievements will multiply and develop in your life if they are well nurtured. Rejoicing as you achieve each and every one of your goals creates the right conditions for future success.

By extending this celebratory feeling towards others – friends, colleagues and work mates – you will also prevent feelings of envy or jealousy from arising. In this way, you guard against attracting negative chi.

If you remember to rejoice in the positive aspects of your life often enough you will succeed in creating an aura of joyousness around you, untainted by any hostile or negative emotions.

# 108 Keep a picture of a beautiful YOU on your dressing table

Images of you looking your best will help you subconsciously to work at retaining those aspects of your appearance.

To improve your self-esteem, look for a photograph of yourself that shows you looking your best and mount it in a frame for your dressing table. Never mind if, at first, your picture seems to look better than the real, every day you. Believe in and celebrate the best you can be. When the first picture of yourself that you see each morning is one that reminds you of how lovely you are – and can continue to be – it boosts your self-image.

### Improve your self-belief

In time you will find your own self-image becomes even more positive than the vision of yourself on your dressing table. This is because you are working on both your physical appearance and inner spiritual strength. The day will come to change the photograph for a more up-to-date image of yourself as, over time, your beauty increases.

### Photograph albums

As you keep the memories of your entire family in your photograph albums always follow the same rules as you would for photographs of yourself. See family events and gatherings like weddings and parties with everyone looking beautiful and happy.

### Keep only auspicious pictures

A cardinal rule of personal feng shui is to delete instantly any pictures that do not flatter you. Never dwell on them, committing the negative image of yourself to mind. Do not keep on file, in photo albums, in frames or even on your computer, images that show you at a bad angle, in unflattering lighting or with a negative expression on your face.

Observe this same rule with every member of your family. In time the records you keep of all the important events in your life will show you looking beautiful, happy and energized. Only show family pictures in which everyone is looking happy to be together, as this translates into reality.

# Place auspicious enhancers on your dressing table    109

The dressing table is one of the most important places to activate with excellent symbolic feng shui images and decorative objects. I love the way cosmetic and fragrance companies spend time, money and effort making their packaging beautiful. This magnifies the good chi that comes from using the products. When you place visually pleasing cosmetics, creams and perfumes on your dressing table, you instantly create an ambience of abundance and style, symbolizing the good life.

## Symbolic lucky objects

By adding other auspicious images to your dressing table you further enhance the ambience of early morning feng shui. Some of the most powerful decorative objects for a dressing table include your astrological allies and secret friend – preferably bejewelled to indicate wealth and prosperity. If you are

Flowers are an ideal enhancer along with wealth-enhancing jewelled decorations.

single, you may also want to place your peach blossom animal on the dressing table to activate a more exciting love life.

## Wish-fulfilling jewels and mirror luck

Look for wish-fulfilling jewels that will add sparkle to your dressing table. Made of either high-quality coloured glass or lead crystals, these are excellent reminders to generate aspirational energy early in the morning. Finally, invest in a good mirror that provides a beautiful frame for your face so that your reflection is auspicious.

Create an impression of wealth and style by placing decorative perfume and cosmetics bottles on your dressing table.

# 110 Keep a picture of a loved one on your dressing table

The bedroom is a good place to have a picture of a loved one. If you are still in the courtship phase of your relationship, place a photograph of your partner on your dressing table. It will generate thoughts of love early in the morning, and there is nothing more powerful for encouraging the relationship

Display happy images of loved ones on your dressing table in the bedroom.

to go smoothly and remain meaningful. If you are married, make sure that the picture you display shows both you and your partner together smiling and looking joyful.

## Show joy to boost joy

In pictures, your loved ones should always appear happy. The expressions on their faces leave a subconscious impression on your mind, generating chi energy. This is known as 'creating imprints in the mind'. A happy face creates a happy imprint and the seed of this, in turn, generates happy aspirations.

Beware, though, that if your dressing area is in the bathroom, you should not follow this advice. This is because images of you or your loved ones should never be placed near the toilet. Only display such images on your dressing table if it is in an auspicious part of the bedroom or, perhaps, in a specially allocated dressing room.

# Make positive statements to your mirror image every morning 111

By reciting powerfully worded affirmation statements about yourself and your desires on a regular basis you are creating your own personal mantras that have an uncanny way of becoming reality. This is especially true when you give voice to them as you look at your own image in the mirror. It is vital to be in a happy, positive state of mind when you do this.

## Focussing on your wishes

Reciting your wishes in front of a mirror is an incredibly potent exercise when it is repeated every morning. It engages both the visual and audio perceptions within your mind, so this ritual has immense power to affect your consciousness at different levels. As your ears and eyes pick up the suggestive elements of your voice and your appearance, these positive messages are transmitted to your subconscious. Here, they act to influence your thought processes and behaviour patterns.

## Boost your positive aura

Affirmations carried out in front of a mirror are an effective way of conditioning yourself so that over time, you will create a very positive aura around yourself This can-do attitude finds its way into the depth of your soul and consciousness, and is vital to your personal success.

Recite your aspirations to yourself every morning as you prepare to face the day.

**ENERGY TIP**

### Be positive to make the most of the auspicious statements you recite

Recite your auspicious statements with confidence and total conviction as to their truth and inevitability. Say them directly to yourself, looking into your own eyes in the mirror. As you do this, imagine that your voice is actually that of your higher self, communicating directly with your conscious self.

# 112    Develop the habit of happiness attitudes

The impact of crowds and aggravating people can be reduced by positive thinking. Wearing red can also help!

While you work at transforming your self-perception – getting rid of doubts and misgivings in order to create a more positive and feel-good 'you' – remember also to work on developing positive mindsets and intrinsic attitudes. Unless you consciously create attitudes of happiness and determinedly strengthen your resolve to be joyous and not to be hostile, whatever the provocation, it is easy to let more negative feelings flourish.

## Accepting disappointments

The path to true happiness lies in your ability to let go if need be, rather than to cling to the outcomes you want. Remember that everyone's life is filled with aggravating people and situations – such as a person who lets you down or a plan that goes awry. How badly you let this affect you depends on yourself and the adaptability of your ego.

## Reducing space hostility

Feng shui practices can help you to reduce the aggravations of space and time hostility afflictions. For example, wear red to your office if you anticipate enduring a difficult meeting. Keeping your home well lit also guards against a build up of negative chi, which results in disagreements and misunderstandings between members of your family.

However, it is also beneficial to do some work on your own attitudes towards life's situations and your reaction to other people. Indeed, by consciously arranging your home in accordance with positive feng shui principles, as well as working on your personal issues, you are taking care of the mankind and earth aspects of the trinity of luck and wellbeing. This adds tremendously to your feelings of wellness and happiness.

# Train to become a person of substance 113

To feel like one is truly a person of substance is at the crux of all success and happiness. Years ago I remember someone asking a candidate in an American presidential election, 'Where's the beef?' The candidate's inability to repudiate this single statement was so telling that it cost him the presidency. Although packaging and hype have become ever-present in modern politics, image cannot be sustained without substance.

### Earn the respect of others

Adopting good feng shui practice will jump start you on the road to long-term success. As you increase your mind's awareness and make a habit of positive thought patterns, you will broaden your knowledge and experience. This hard work brings lasting success and recognition and there is no short cut. The respect of others must be earned and does not come by magic. The good news is, of course, that real substance is within reach of everybody who is willing to put in conscious effort to achieve it.

### Work on yourself

A happy, successful life is not something confined only to an elite few. We each have the capability to become expert at the things we do if we only take the trouble to improve ourselves. The contemporary work scene is becoming increasingly competitive, as many already know. The best way to cope with its demands is to work at strengthening your inner self and improving your outer charisma, while becoming the best you can be at what you do.

Only by broadening both your knowledge and experience will you be able to achieve success and recognition.

Enjoy the recognition of others when it has been earned by hard work: it is within the reach of us all.

# 114 Think of yourself as a charismatic genius – and you will become one

Success in life is never the result of effort alone. It is always combined with the power of believing in yourself. Never allow debilitating doubts to sap your courage or belittle your confidence.

There is an old adage that says that you are a genius if you believe that you are. It also states that, if you are convinced you are a charismatic genius, then you will be more than just a clever soul – you will also be recognized as such. Recognition is, of course, key because the world is full of unrecognized geniuses.

Feng shui practice is a valuable life skill because, with a knowledge of just the simple feng shui tools, you can enhance your recognition corner at the same time as you work on building your expertise and confidence. The knowledge that you are doing everything you can to realize your dreams and ambitions is empowering in itself.

**Have faith in yourself**

Intrinsic to the practice of believing is having faith in yourself, and in those who want to help and support you in what you do. Vital to genius is the ability to work with others and to recognize their unique talents. Arrogance has no place in this way of thinking. True charisma is self-confidence without a hint of arrogance. Think about this statement in relation to charismatic people, upon whose shoulders success and fame sits easily.

You must trust the power of your beliefs to enhance your recognition corner.

# Create an aura of success around you    115

Create an ambience of success around yourself. By this, I do not mean what public-relations specialists and publicists call 'packaging' – promoting yourself with much rhetoric in order to gain recognition and respect. However, I do advocate rehearsing your own life story inside your mind. Focus exclusively on all your positive attainments and praiseworthy deeds. Remember that there is a right way and wrong way to tell the story of your life – the happy, inspiring way that reflects your successes will lead the way to more good fortune in the future.

## Develop positive thinking

It may take time to adapt to seeing yourself in this positive light. However, as you search through the memory banks of your mind, bringing out the best aspects of your own story, remembering real evidence of your strengths and talents, you will unknowingly be creating an aura of success around yourself. This is a worthwhile exercise because many people find it all too easy to dwell on failures and disappointments, and will find it especially beneficial to develop a new, positive habit of thinking.

## The power of a positive aura

The aura, or energy field, surrounding you determines how others react to you. When your aura is powerful and uplifting, the reaction of everyone who comes into contact

with you will be very positive in a way that transcends verbal communication. Think about the people you know whose very presence enhances your mood and confidence. This is what charisma is all about – the ability to be memorable to others and to inspire others to seek their highest goals.

Creating an aura of success also attracts real success into your life. It is an uncanny phenomenon which, when it first happens, will surprise you. Over time, however, you will become used to expecting magic to happen in all your endeavours. You will come to realize that success is a self-fulfilling wish that we can all embrace.

Let the positive power of your aura touch all those you come into contact with.

# 116 Surround your space with happy images

Use happy reminders of your children to encourage chi energy into the home.

Filling your home with decorative objects associated with moments of happiness from your life is one of the most powerful methods of creating auspicious chi energy. Happy images can be beautiful paintings or embroideries or objects that touch a particular chord within you. Alternatively, they can be simply photographs of people who bring you joy. By decorating

your space with only objects and images that please you visually, you are creating you own style and form of feng shui magic.

**Throw away your bad luck**

Throw out everything that has unhappy, negative or disturbing associations. The act of discarding such items has the powerful impact of literally getting rid of bad luck and people from your life.

# 117 Always wear alluring scents

Use perfume to stimulate the senses.

Wear beautiful or uplifting scents. These stimulate your sense of smell and, in so doing, heighten the effectiveness of the middle zone of your face.

**Activate mind and body communication**

Dab spots of perfume at the power points of your body. These are the spots behind your eyes, on the insides of your upper arms and on the insides of your wrists. Some people refer to these as pressure points. They are the places through which your mind and body can communicate, as the scent stimulates the evocative sense of smell.

# Practise important morning rituals 118

Look upon the morning as a beautiful and auspicious beginning to an active, fulfilled and meaningful day. Try to capture the Hour of the Dragon (from 7am to 9am) when the morning's majestic yang energy is at full strength. If you sleep through this time, you are letting this revitalizing energy go to waste. Try to be up and about so you can enjoy the special, invigorating morning air.

Early morning meditation during the Hour of the Dragon encourages yang energy to enter your mind and body. This gives you mental and spiritual vitality that will keep you energized throughout the day.

## Enjoy the cool of the day

Early morning is the time when yang energy is young. The sun's rays are gentle, and the heat of the day has not yet become oppressive because the cool of the night still lingers. This is the best time to perform all your important morning rituals – some people workout, some do tai chi or yoga, while others meditate.

## Stay centred and beautiful

These morning rituals help keep you centred to the cosmic energy of the Universe. For example, you might start the day with a refreshing wash before meditating in the early morning rays of the sun. Meditating, you can feel your own purity and beauty in the presence of the divine, as uplifting yang energy enters your body and gives a wonderful boost to start your day.

### ENERGY TIP

## Early morning meditation

Before meditating it is helpful to have a bath or shower, then wear some of your precious jewellery, even some sparkling 'bling'. Contrary to popular belief, it is not best to meditate wearing loose clothes or to be devoid of all make-up and jewels. Try the following meditation to get your day off to an excellent start: close your eyes lightly and let your mind transport you to the Garden of Eden. Here, imagine yourself meeting with beautiful Goddesses and magical Dakinis. Let their goodness, purity and divinity enter your soul and energize your being.

# Chapter Six

# Re-energizing and Updating Your Living Space

Every New Year we need to update the arrangement of furniture and the placement of cures and enhancers to counter the ever-changing annual afflictions. This means getting acquainted with feng shui remedies and cures as well as knowing some useful feng shui tips on decorating with colours; selecting decorative objects and finding art that also has auspicious meaning. Placed correctly, these luck-bringing items bring yang chi into rooms.

Let your mind and your inner spirit work together to form a strong partnership to transform the energy of your physical space as you update its energies. If your mind is focused every time you make changes or place cures, your mind will connect with the space – bringing balance and focus to your feng shui. It then becomes easy to manifest all the aspirations of each New Year, from experiencing a more active social life to improving your business networking.

# Reactivate the energy cycles of your home. 119

Time is divided into three 60-year cycles, with each 12-year cycle beginning with the year of the Rat. Overlapping this cycle is the flying star cycle of periods, in which each period of time has its own powerful designated number. There are nine period numbers from 1 to 9, and in each period a single number dominates – this number is also the luckiest number throughout the 20 years that make up each single period.

The current period number is 8 – its 20-year period began on February 4 2004. As 8 is already a lucky number in feng shui this period of 8 makes even more powerful its ability to bring good fortune to all, confirming the huge popularity of 8 both as a number and symbol of good fortune.

## Charting change

In feng shui nothing is static and everything is dynamic: energy cycles ebb and flow according to changes in the environment. While it may only be practical to monitor the time changes each year (or perhaps each month), in truth changes in energy cycles happen over the course of each day and even from moment to moment. The ancient feng shui soothsayers of China spent their lives charting these changes, always on the lookout for the big blips that mark significant events or changes of fortune or the hugely strong alignment of a particular good number with an evil number in a single moment of time. These are the moments astrologers look for as being points of great significance when very good or very bad things happen in the locations of the world where such congregations of numbers occur.

The Rat marks the beginning of the 12-year cycle of years in Chinese astrology. In flying star feng shui, each cycle lasts for 20 years.

The purpose of studying the numbers was always to be forewarned of cosmic afflictions so that the knowledge of feng shui and its different formulas could overcome the portents of danger and afflictions. This, too, should be the motivation for wanting to know about the changes of chi energy and how these affect us personally, in our individual homes and rooms. Being aware of the time changes of energy are vital and important aspects of feng shui practice.

## Incorporating flying star feng shui

Indeed, you may have a very well-designed house that conforms to all the feng shui 'rules', yet you could well suffer severely in a year when time afflictions fly into your bedroom or hurt the space around your front door. The bad luck of time-dimension feng shui manifests as severe misfortune and hostility. Quarrelsome energies can break up relationships or cause debilitating illnesses that bring heartache to a household.

When you know how to update the feng shui of your home each year this complements your spatial practice, thereby improving its effectiveness substantially.

# 120 Updating feng shui starts every February 4th

February 4 is New Year's Day based on the Hsia solar calendar, but monthly dates in the Hsia calendar and the more traditional Lunar calendar can vary by up to a few days. Many people are unaware that the Chinese follow two calendars, just as few realize that advanced feng shui practitioners follow three measurements of the direction north.

### The Hsia and Lunar calendars

In measuring time, therefore, be prepared to use both Hsia and Lunar calendars because different formulas use different calendars when measuring time. Unfortunately, even when using the same calendar not every geomancer is agreed on the start and end dates of the Chinese year so don't allow yourself to get confused. When tracking time changes of energy I have also discovered that sometimes the indicated misfortune or good fortune can start slightly earlier or later than expected. The measurement of time is still an imperfect tool but in practice we need not get too hung up on this: if an affliction is diagnosed, be prepared and take precautions well in advance!

Decorated lampshades adorn the streets to mark the New Year. Their red colour gives out strong yang energy.

### The luckiest day

In practice, though, you should use February 4 as the starting point not only for updating your feng shui but also for reading your fortunes and luck potential based on Chinese astrological charts. The day also marks the start of spring, known as the day of the lap chun. It is generally regarded as a very lucky day. If, however, you wish to determine what animal sign you are, use the Lunar calendar as this is the calendar used in feng shui astrology.

Children in traditional dress celebrate Chinese New Year.

# Locating areas of affliction each New Year  121

The areas of afflicted chi energy in any building or demarcated space each year are revealed in the annual flying star feng shui chart (see right). The chart shows the compass directions of your home, so that you will see at a glance which areas will need special attention due to changes in the nature of chi energy in those spaces. If you wish, you could also overlay an annual chart on a floor-plan in order to identify lucky and unlucky locations for each floor of your home, or for particular rooms in which you spend a lot of time.

## Make your changes early

Each year you need to locate the areas of affliction and the areas of auspicious chi that will affect your home – these energy differences are potent and powerful and explain changes in people's attitudes and people's luck, as well as the luck of houses and buildings. Whatever changes you make to your home, ideally you should make them right at the start of the New Year in February: attending to these afflictions before they can begin to exert their effect will make a world of difference to your luck throughout the whole year.

Updating your space this way requires you to use the correct natal chart of the year. For the charts of future years visit the author's website just before the new year is due to get the updates.

## Revealing flying star secrets

In the past, the flying star chart was only revealed and discussed in some of the annual Chinese Almanacs, usually followed by many

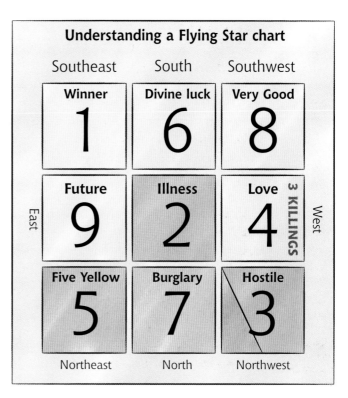

An annual flying star chart indicates the areas of your home that will both suffer from annual afflictions and benefit from auspicious chi. In this example for 2007, the afflictions all flew to the northern and central points of the chart. For annual updates, go to www.wofs.com each New Year.

traditionalists. However, recently much of this all-important information has been brought to the notice of the English-speaking world through my annual fortune and feng shui astrology books, and also my magazine and website. Over a number of years, a great deal of information on this subject has been gathered and archived on the website.

You can visit the site to view and download these flying star updates free, which become available each Chinese New Year around the month of February.

# 122 Suppressing the five yellow star of misfortune

| Five Yellow | Burglary |
|---|---|
| ⭐5 | 7 |
| NORTHEAST | NORTH |

In 2007 the wu wang, or 'five yellow' flew to the northeast. In 2008 it flies to the south, and in 2009 it resides in the north.

cause of career stagnation, obstacles blocking opportunities and success, and illnesses taking a turn for the worse. Regarded as an evil star, the wu wang is indicated by the number 5 so when you look at the annual chart the first thing to identify is the location of the number 5. In 2007, for example, the wu wang flew to the northeast sector, afflicting this direction of your house and rooms. In 2008 the wu wang is in the south and in the north in 2009. In 2010, the wu wang flies to the southwest.

Probably the most powerful misfortune star indicated by the annual flying star chart is the 'five yellow', also known as the wu wang. The misfortunes it is capable of bringing vary according to the personal luck of people as well as the luck of the house itself. But, by and large, the wu wang affliction brings illness, accidents, misfortunes, tragedies, betrayals and just about anything that might go wrong with your life. The wu wang is the principal

## Countering the 'five yellow'

Each New Year, it is important to determine the wu wang's location in the home and then place remedies in the afflicted locations – these are the five-element pagoda and all-metal, six-rod windchimes. Also, do take note that wherever the wu wang resides in any year, the area should be kept dimly lit and all crystals and crystal geodes or energizers should be removed.

# Controlling the star of illness affliction  123

The illness star brings with it the affliction of illness and disease. This is not usually the simple cold or cough but instead is something more severe. It is really bad news when the illness star flies into your bedroom because it is while you are sleeping that you are the most vulnerable so the illness star can really play havoc with your health.

### Find the illness star

If the illness star 2 falls where your bedroom is located, the danger of illness could befall you. However, if the illness star falls on a corridor or store room, it becomes less of a threat. If the illness star flies to the centre of the chart then the whole world should become wary of the rise of epidemics and the spread of other kinds of disease. In 2007 the illness star dominated the centre of the flying star chart. In 2008 it afflicts the northwest, and flies to the west in 2009. By 2010, the illness star will reside in the northeast.

### Retain your health

If the illness star falls into a part of the home where there is a big space then the chi of illness is strengthened. This will require a massive dose of cures and remedies, the best of which is metal energy. Combine this with the divine deities associated with health and medicines, such as the Medicine Buddha, the Mandala of the Medicine Buddha and the universal Chinese symbol of good health – the wu lou, especially if it includes images of the Eight Immortals or of the herbal medicines associated with getting well.

The wu lou is the Chinese symbol of good health and is an effective remedy for the illness star, which is number 2 on a flying star chart. Each year, move the wu lou to the afflicted location. Ideally, buy a new wu lou each year to bring in fresh, new energy.

## How to assess an area of affliction

The area affected by the illness star in this house mainly covers a corridor so it is less problematic. If in future years it flies to a corner containing a bedroom, you will need to place a wu lou there to reduce the star's ability to cause sickness to the room's occupants.

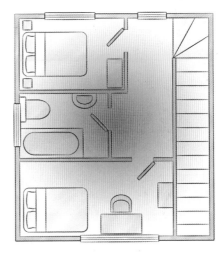

# 124 Protect against being the victim of hostile behaviour

Another very fearsome affliction indicated by the flying star chart is the hostility star. This is usually one of the most severe and hard-to-bear afflictions as it can cause people to turn against you for no apparent reason. This is the star of quarrelsome energy, which brings misunderstandings, generates hostile behaviour and generally creates bad feelings through a house. In severe cases the affliction can bring court cases and legal entanglements, which are not only aggravating but will also drain you of vigour and energy. What can be done about such a terrible affliction?

*Use the colours red, for fire, and gold, representing metal, to counter the number 3 star.*

## Fight with fire

Feng shui's answer to this troublesome and quarrelsome star, which is usually brought by the number 3 in the annual chart, is to overcome it with fire energy. Yes, the cure for the hostile fighting star is the colour red, which will work even better when accompanied by metal (or gold) energy. Somehow the presence of gold and red together effectively suppresses the hostility energy. You could display a red mandala painting, for example, a laughing Buddha wearing red robes or a six-ring staff of Ksiddhigarbha (see Tips 146 and 148).

## Where will it be?

In the year 2007 the number 3 star was in the northwest. In 2008 it is located in the west and in 2009, the north-east. The hostility star flies to the south in 2010. If your room or your front door are located in these sectors, you must install enough remedies to counter the hostility star. This will ensure that you do not become the unwitting victim of unreasonable, hostile anger – anger is the main emotion unleashed by the number 3 star, so make sure you are adequately safe-guarded against it by installing proper cures. Do take this affliction seriously as it may potentially lead to violence and tragedy.

# Safeguard homes from burglars and from being cheated  125

You can also safeguard against getting burgled, robbed and cheated in a year by updating your feng shui. Each year the burglary star flies into a different part of a dwelling, and when it strikes where your front door and back doors are located, it activates the burglary star for your home.

Although the number 7 burglary star brings violence to the affected location it can be overcome with relatively simple cures – the elephant and the blue rhinoceros.

**Burglary**
**7**

**NORTH**

## Prepare yourself

This is part of flying star feng shui updating that you simply cannot ignore or treat lightly. At the start of each year you should take precautions against being robbed. And, because the burglary star is the number 7 in the chart, it also implies violence accompanied by bloodshed – not at all pleasant if this affliction strikes you.

## The blue rhinoceros

The cure is the blue rhino – one with a double horn is most effective. In 2008 the burglary star is in the southwest and in 2009, the north-east. If any of your doors is located in these sectors, place a blue rhino beside them or, alternatively, an elephant. A figurine about 45 cm (18 inches) high, with its trunk raised, is poised to protect and counter any hostile moves against you. An elephant with the trunk down is benevolent, and enhances fertility and descendants' luck.

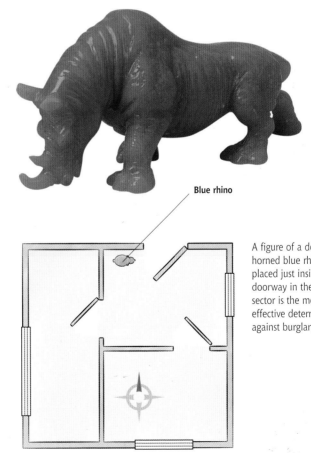

Blue rhino

A figure of a double-horned blue rhino placed just inside a doorway in the afflicted sector is the most effective deterrent against burglary.

# 126 Getting support from the Tai Sui or Year God

Place a Pi Yao figurine in the presence of the Tai Sui to protect against his wrath and ensure his support.

Ensure you give special attention to the Tai Sui, or Grand Duke Jupiter, at the start of each New Year. Followers of time dimension feng shui are always particularly mindful not to offend the Tai Sui. In the schools of feng shui followed by Hong Kong masters even greater prominence is given to the Tai Sui, who is regarded as the God of the year. The masters believe that inadvertently offending the Tai Sui leads instantly to misfortune befalling the household.

Any digging, cutting or other very loud renovations disturbing the sector of the house where the Tai Sui resides during the year will cause offence. Since his residence changes from year to year, you need to find out where he is so that you can remove all televisions, radios and other disturbing equipment. During New Year celebrations, you should not even let off firecrackers near Tai Sui's residence.

## Safeguard against bad luck

The location of the Tai Sui or Grand Duke is also a taboo facing direction. If you choose to sit directly facing the Tai Sui you are described as 'confronting the Tai Sui' and this brings enormous losing luck. You cannot enjoy any kind of success when facing the Tai Sui, even if that is your best personal luck direction based upon other feng shui formulas.

To appease the Tai Sui the best remedy is to call on the celestial creature Pi Yao, the pet of the Tai Sui. Placing the Pi Yao in the Tai Sui's presence not only pleases him, thus protecting against misfortune, but also brings wealth luck into the home.

## ENERGY TIP

### Locating the Tai Sui

To know where the Tai Sui resides each year just remember that he follows the animal sign of the year. Hence in 2007, the year of the Pig, the Tai Sui was in the northwest 3 direction. In 2008 the Tai Sui is in the south 2 location and in 2009 he moves to the northeast 1 location. In 2010 the Tai Sui resides in northeast 3. In fact, each year he moves 30 degrees in a clockwise direction around the astrological wheel.

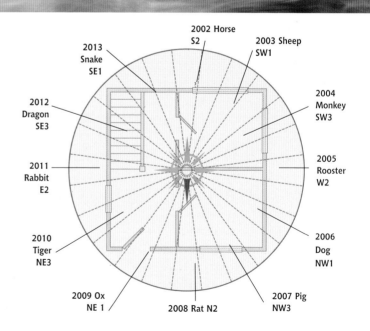

2002 Horse S2
2003 Sheep SW1
2013 Snake SE1
2004 Monkey SW3
2012 Dragon SE3
2005 Rooster W2
2011 Rabbit E2
2006 Dog NW1
2010 Tiger NE3
2007 Pig NW3
2009 Ox NE 1
2008 Rat N2

# Shielding your home from the Three Killings 127

The Three Killings is one of the 'special stars' that fly in the directions that make up the 24 'mountains' of the compass. An affliction star, the Three Killings always flies in one of the four cardinal directions – north, south, east or west – and it changes location in your home from year to year. To guard against the ill luck brought about by the Three Killings, it is useful to find out each year where it is.

## Three kinds of misfortune

The misfortunes brought by the Three Killings to whoever lives in the part of the house that the star flies to are mainly related to loss – loss of your good name, loss of love and/or friendship and loss of money. However, you can suppress the strength of the Three Killings and safeguard yourself and your family from its influence by placing the three celestial guardians in appropriate locations.

## Three celestial guardians

The Fu dog, the Chi lin and the Pi Yao are celestial creatures, sent to Earth by the God of Heaven to safeguard the trinity of tien ti ren. The Chinese have depended upon the divine powers of these protectors for thousands of years.

Placing three-dimensional images of the divine protectors near your main door, or in the afflicted sector of your home, invokes their spiritual presence and creates a safeguard for all residents. Chi lin (dragon horses) are often thought to be the best protection against the Three Killings. It is therefore a good idea to keep Chi lin in the sector of your home afflicted by the star.

Keep a pair of Fu dogs as a protective symbol, placing them either at the front door looking out or in the location affected by the Three Killings.

## ENERGY TIP
### Locating the Three Killings

To discover the location of the Three Killings, note the ruling animal sign of that year. In 2007, the Three Killings was in the west, and it will also be here during the Rabbit, Boar and Sheep years. In 2008 the Three Killings will be in the south, where

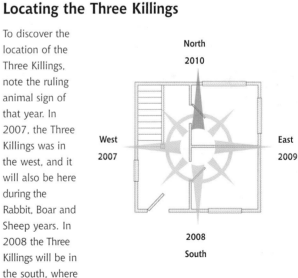

it is located during the years of the Rat, the Monkey and the Dragon. In 2009 the location of the Three Killings moves to the east and this is where it will be during the years of the Rooster, the Snake and the Ox. In 2010 the Three Killings moves to the north, and it will also be here during the years of the Tiger, Horse and Dog.

# 128 Change furniture arrangement once a year

This is one of the best and easiest ways of moving energy around, allowing stale and tired energy to be released. Once a year, just before February 4, choose a good day for spring-cleaning. Move every piece of furniture in each room away from its usual spot. Vacuum and clean the exposed spaces thoroughly. Either move the furniture back to its previous position or seize the opportunity to rearrange it. Not only does this start energy moving, but it is an efficient way to re-energize all the rooms in your home.

## A positive mood affects energy

Make sure you are in a happy, positive frame of mind with nothing disturbing you. Vibes from a bad mood stick to the energy of your home. If you move furniture around when you are feeling anxious, angry or aggrieved you will do more harm than good.

When you move larger pieces of furniture it is a good idea to enlist the help of a family member or friend – so long as that person is happy to assist and so sends out good vibes.

**Planning a new room layout**

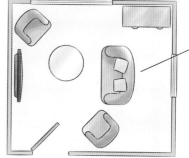

In this layout the seating arrangement mainly faces away from the window side of the room in an auspicious direction for the previous year.

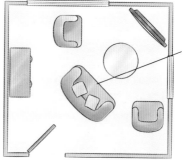

The seating still allows space for the flow of chi but is angled around to face in an auspicious direction for the coming year.

## Dispelling negative chi

Moving furniture in your home is also something you can do when your luck seems to be especially bad. If you have been hit by a series of setbacks or misfortunes, go for an 'instant fix' by rearranging the furniture in the rooms that you spend a lot of time in.

Personally, just before New Year I always rearrange the furniture in my living areas as well as inside my study. As well as allowing me to update my directions this also releases all the past year's energy.

# Enhance lucky corners with auspicious objects 129

The Chinese are great believers in the power of symbolic feng shui. Deities, divine celestial creatures, heavenly symbols, trees, flowers and all kinds of shapes and colours possess a variety of auspicious meanings. In practice, inspiration is taken from the I Ching (the Book of Changes) where symbols of broken and unbroken lines have powerful connotations. Knowledge of the meaning of these symbols, and their relationship with the five elements, provides enlightenment for the practice of symbolic feng shui.

A pair of brass Chi lin is not only auspicious but a safeguard against bad luck befalling the household.

A pair of mandarin ducks placed in the Southwest sector activate love and good relationship luck.

## Locating lucky corners

Symbolic objects have most power when they are placed in the lucky corners of your home. Each year different parts of your home become auspicious. Keep yourself up to date with where lucky corners are, using a compass to locate them. This allows you to increase your fortune chi for the year.

## Activating different energies

Selecting auspicious objects for lucky corners can be confusing due to a number of feng shui formulas recommending a variety of elements and objects for different corners. However, it is perfectly good practice to place multiple objects in any corner to enhance different dimensions of luck.

In 2008, for example, the east – a wood corner – is very auspicious. To activate its flying star good fortune, use the water element to jump-start wealth luck. As the east is also the place of the eldest son, you can enhance good fortune for the sons of the family by placing a symbol of a young man there. According to the Eight Aspirations Pa Kua formula, the east brings good health and family luck, so you can also place the wu lou here (see Tip 123). This example demonstrates the many layers of meaning that can be given to each of the eight compass sectors. The luckiest sector in 2009 is the southeast, also a wood corner, and in 2010 it is the centre of the chart, which benefits everyone in the home.

## Creative thinking

Be imaginative in fine-tuning your feng shui practice to activate all the auspicious corners of your home without overwhelming it with too many symbolic objects. For example, you might place water in the east corner of your garden, or place the wu lou in the east corner of your bedroom.

# 130 Energize quiet corners and dispel bad chi with sound

When your home has more yin time than yang time you need to compensate – homes always benefit from the presence of life, or yang energy, so ask yourself how best you can achieve this. One way is to use the revitalizing effects of sound, which dispels negative or stagnant energy. High notes are more yang while low notes are more yin. The ideal is a combination of both.

If your home is empty all day long, create sound energy while you are out by keeping the television, radio or stereo on. It is also a great idea to hang a windchime in a quiet corner to energize the space and thereby guard against the accumulation of harmful chi. Hang the windchime near a flow of breeze, such as by a window. Do not sit directly under a windchime or hang it above a door, however.

To overcome a build-up of yin in or around your home, there is nothing more effective than metal energy. For this reason metal windchimes, such as these brass bells, are more effective than wooden ones.

# 131 Create yang energy in your home with activity

According to the classical feng shui texts, we enjoy good energy when we achieve the balance of tien ti ren within our homes. Heaven energy, earth energy and mankind energy must all be present for good feng shui. Of the three kinds of energy, it is mankind energy that is most important in creating a revitalizing and restorative home.

**Avoiding excessive yin build-up**

If you and your partner have high-energy careers, eating out and coming home only to sleep, your home will become excessively yin. If this happens, you must make an effort to activate yang energy, otherwise your careers will start to stagnate and problems will occur in your relationship. Try to eat at home more often so that activity, conversation and laughter creates yang energy. It is also really beneficial to keep pets such as dogs or cats in your home, or to have an older relative to stay with you.

Create sound with a television.

# Activate your home with lights for better luck 132

I always advise keeping a house well lit, as this attracts auspicious yang energy. A great way to double the benefits of annually updating the auspicious parts of your home is to activate an auspicious object, such as a horse, a dragon or a wu lou, with lights. Shining lights on your symbolic enhancers is a sure way of energizing them.

## Increase lighting in your home

Many cities are more brightly lit than ever before. Singapore, Kuala Lumpur and Hong Kong are illuminated at night by lots of twinkling lights, and there is no doubt that these create much better feng shui. Well-lit shopping malls and restaurants also enjoy much better business. To improve your luck, increase the number of lights in your home. During festive seasons, decorate your rooms

Cities illuminated by bright lights counteract the yin of nighttime with yang energy.

For special occasions in particular, energize your home with as many lights as possible – tealights make pretty table decorations.

with as many Christmas lights as possible, lighting up the south and southwest corners.

In 2008, fire energy is missing from the year's chart, so bright lights become even more effective at this time.

# 133 Re-dot the eyes of your celestial guardians with cinnabar

If you cannot find a red cinnabar stick, use a narrow-tipped brush dipped in red paint.

This is a Taoist ritual for revitalizing your home's celestial guardians. I flank every entrance door with guardian protectors – Fu dogs and Chi lins – as I believe they have a protective aura that prevents people with bad intentions from entering my home. Each year I re-energize my celestial guardians with this powerful ritual.

Using cinnabar red paint, I re-dot the eyes of my guardians, and I give them a new pair of ribbons and pompoms. The act of dotting their eyes makes them even more alert for the coming year. Once every three years I also invite a Taoist master to undertake this re-energizing ritual and to check for me whether the celestial guardians need replacing. If you cannot find red cinnabar then use ordinary red paint. Any kind of enamel paint will do but never use watercolour paint as this fades easily.

## Keep guardians in good condition

I am often asked whether feng shui protectors and guardians remain effective year after year and I have to say that this depends on whether they are still in good condition. If you find a chip in a guardian, or a broken part of the body, then it is better to replace it.

If you have inherited a feng shui celestial guardian, or you buy an antique, they can be re-energized and will be even more powerful if they are in good condition with no chips, breaks or repairs.

# 134 Protecting the energy of the matriarch

The southwest corner of the home symbolizes powerful matriarchal energy, reflecting the level of nurturing that a home benefits from. The importance of the mother figure in feng shui can never be overstressed. It is she who ensures that a family stays together and grows together.

In feng shui, the matriarchal energy also creates family harmony and romance luck. When the presence of fire and earth energy – through light and crystal – activates the southwest corners of your home, the matriarch is tremendously empowered. This brings luck and success to the home and its residents. In the current period of eight, which ends in 2024, the southwest corner benefits from the presence of water. If there is a pond, fountain or other type of water feature in this location, it will bring prosperity to the household easily.

## Beware wood energy

Take care not to have too many plants or trees in the southwest corner because wood energy harms the earth energy of the southwest. If the mother is threatened by illness or depression, remove all the wood energy from the corner. Instead, install lights, a light-coloured tree or a chandelier here. Fire energy benefits the matriarch.

Fire energy always activates the earth element of the southwest corner.

# Open doors and windows every New Moon day 135

This is a wonderful ritual to follow every time the New Moon appears, bringing fresh new energy into your home. Look in the feng shui almanac to see when the day of the New Moon occurs and, on that day, open the doors and windows of every room. If the day is sunny, the energy for the coming 30 days will be bright and infused with yang chi. If the day is dark and cloudy, the outlook is not as promising because of the infusion of yin energy. On a Full Moon day, it is a great omen when the day's energy is predominantly yang.

## Re-energizing with incense

When you follow this ritual of opening your doors to let in cosmic chi, you are regularly cleansing and purifying your living space. You can also use incense to re-energize your home. It heightens the intensity of new energy, and is particularly recommended for households where the inhabitants feel depressed or have been suffering from a bout of misfortune luck.

Using an incense burner intensifies new yang energy.

## The waxing and waning Moon

Early in the evening on the first day of a New Moon and 15 days thereafter, consciously invite its revitalizing energy into your home and open your doors and windows. After this comes 15 days of the waning Moon, when the supply of energy becomes depleted.

If the day of a Full Moon is sunny, let in fresh yang energy by opening windows and doors.

# 136 Paying particular attention to the place of the patriarch

The northwest corner of the home symbolizes the patriarch. In houses where the northwest corner is missing, it is likely that the patriarch is also missing for much of the time. He may, for example, travel a great deal for his work or work late on a regular basis. In houses where the northwest corner is missing, I am never surprised to hear that the man of the house has taken up with another woman. A missing northwest corner leads to this kind of situation. If, as well as a missing northwest corner, there are other afflictions to the home, the patriarch may even die. In a work setting, the absence of the northwest corner indicates a lack of leadership within the organization.

A missing northwest corner can be hard to remedy unless there is a way to extend the home or office, literally building the corner.

## Avoid afflictions in the northwest

Afflictions in the northwest corner can cause as much damage as a missing corner. Locate the northwest corner of your home and make sure that it does not house a store room – especially one full of junk – a toilet or, worst of all, a kitchen. These are all bad feng shui and will have an adverse effect on the family's patriarch.

Symbolic of the patriarch, the northwest corner of your home will benefit from metal energy – this may be supplied by a practical object such as a fan.

### ENERGY TIP
### Using metal energy

To create good feng shui for the patriarch in your home, strengthen the northwest corners of the living room, study and bedroom with metal energy – the element that signifies the patriarch. It is also beneficial to place a good photograph of the patriarch here as this will strengthen his chi energy. Adding a crystal geode is also empowering.

# Cover exposed shelves in vital corners 137

Take care not to have any exposed shelves in southwest and northwest corners of your home as these indicate knives cutting into the matriarchal and patriarchal energies.

This feng shui affliction is quite common in home offices where exposed shelves are often built behind the desk. Always keep this part of the office clear of fixtures, Instead, it is auspicious to have a clean wall on which to hang a painting of a mountain. If there are exposed shelves here and you need them for storing files and books, build doors to keep the shelves hidden from view.

## Protect your back from poison arrows

It is a golden rule of feng shui always to protect your back from poison arrows. Make sure that shelves do not have protruding edges that directly hit your back. They will act like knives or spears, sending harmful energy into you and causing you to be cheated and stabbed in the back – even by friends and people you trust.

Covering shelves with doors featuring smooth, bevelled edges, as well as handles that do not jut out, is an excellent compromise solution for home offices.

# Use plants to block off sharp edges and 138 shield you from poison arrows

Looking out for poison arrows inside the home is very basic feng shui, yet it is something that many eager-beaver practitioners of advanced feng shui completely forget to do. This often leads to awful misfortunes and illnesses for residents. It is vital to look around your home and take note of any sharp edges – they will nearly always be present. One of the easiest and most effective ways to block off sharp edges is to use leafy plants.

Plants are ideal for screening sharp edges around your home so that you are not struck by poison arrows.

## Hiding hostile exposed beams

It is easy to become so familiar with your home that you are 'blind' to the secret poison arrows occurring in every room. This is especially true of old houses where exposed overhead beams are common. If you live in a home where there is a row of dark black beams above you constantly, consider fitting a ceiling to hide them from view. If you do not want to go this far, some kind of camouflage is still a good idea – you can be as creative as you wish.

# 139 Shine a bright light upwards near the entrance

To enhance the yang energy near the entrance of a home or office it is most beneficial to shine a bright light upwards to lift the energy. This is also a very effective cure for any ailment that is afflicting your door. An upward-shining light always symbolizes young yang energy – excellent for creating good luck. As the front door area is the facing palace of your home, keeping this space well lit enhances the beneficial effects of a bright hall.

## Remedy for a narrow hall

If your home has a restricted facing palace, it is liable to become gloomy and gather yin energy. In this case shining a bright light upwards is a particularly good way to make the space much more auspicious. Cosmic chi is attracted to a bright entrance, from where it flows into the home to refresh it with yang energy.

*A wide facing palace bathed in natural daylight will bring yang energy into the home. Light shining upwards near the front door further intensifies uplifting, positive chi.*

# 140 One or more crystal balls activate the nurturing chi of mother earth

One of the most popular Taoist methods of removing family aggravation is to display crystal balls, which symbolize earth energy. Large, solid crystal balls are most effective as they smooth out tough obstacles that can manifest as relationship problems and blocks to the successful completion of projects. Crystal balls simulate the nurturing energy of mother earth; fashioned into a circular shape, they invoke the blessings of cosmic heaven. There is something very magical about crystal balls even when they are not made from natural crystal.

*Display one, six or eight crystal balls on your coffee table for family harmony.*

Ideally, display six crystal balls, as this symbolizes the energy of heaven. If you cannot afford crystal, use glass balls – they are also extremely effective. You could also have eight balls, instead of six, to capture the power of eight for the current period. Alternatively, have just one very large crystal ball.

## Auspicious numbers

Numbers one, six and eight are particularly suited to the earth energy of crystal. Eight is the most auspicious of the three. The number six is the number of heaven, or big metal, which produces earth. One is the number of water, which is associated with income and prosperity. All three numbers activate the nurturing chi of the cosmic mother.

# A bowl of red apples brings harmony to the home 141

Can you believe that simply placing a bowl of red apples in the hall, living room or dining room enhances the harmony of your home? This is because the apple symbolizes peace while the colour red has the power to dispel hostile energy in the air.

## Remedy for quarrelsome families

Red apples combine the power of red with the power of peace. Those of you who come from large families where sibling rivalry and constant bickering is a problem might find this simple domestic cure especially beneficial. Place the bowl of apples in the room where disagreements most often occur – the dining room table might be a good spot.

Change the apples regularly as sour or bad fruit gives out harmful chi, causing energy to stagnate. It is all too easy for the positive effect of red apples to turn negative if you neglect them.

Juicy red apples are an easy way to introduce peaceful, positive energy.

# Pak choi – 100 types of luck in your home 142

The Chinese have always loved the symbolism of 100 kinds of good fortune. In Chinese, 100 means 'abundance in infinity' so 100 is always used to spell extraordinary good fortune.

The best symbol for gaining the 100 kinds of good fortune is the white cabbage, or pak choi. Display an image of this vegetable prominently in the home so everyone can see it as soon as they walk inside. When someone compliments you on it, this activates the pak choi's benefits. In past times the mandarins and upper classes of Chinese society always displayed a decorative pak choi in their homes. Carved out of green and white jade, these decorative objects were extremely prized.

In contemporary times these symbols of good fortune are made of crystal and coloured resin. They look just as good and work as well as their jade counterparts.

Symbolic of the 100 kinds of good fortune, the pak choi has been considered lucky in China for centuries. Displaying a decorative version of the vegetable in your hall is very auspicious.

# 143 Place Horse images in the south to gain recognition

Inviting images of the horse into your home simultaneously invites in the star of the nobleman. While the horse brings recognition and promotion, the nobleman brings prosperity. Add images of the horse to the south corner of your home to bring in extremely beneficial energy. The Horse is auspicious in the south in all years, so it's always good feng shui to have a Horse in this location – although it is a good idea to change your Horse figurine from time to time to update the energy.

For those born in the years of the Rooster, Snake and Ox, the Horse is a peach blossom luck animal. This means that having a Horse in the south – especially during a year in which the Horse enjoys good luck – will bring love, marriage and enduring happiness.

Having a Horse in the south of the living room, or the south of the bedroom, often brings the luck of fame and good name. A monkey sitting on the horse signifies promotion and upward mobility luck.

Images of the horse are always best placed in the south corner of your home.

**Birth years of the Rooster, the Snake and the Ox**

| Rooster | Snake | Ox |
|---------|-------|------|
| 1933 | 1933 | 1925 |
| 1945 | 1941 | 1937 |
| 1957 | 1953 | 1949 |
| 1969 | 1965 | 1961 |
| 1981 | 1977 | 1973 |
| 1993 | 1989 | 1985 |
| 2005 | 2001 | 1997 |

To find out if the Horse is your peach-blossom animal, refer to the table above. There is more about peach-blossom animals in Tip 164.

# Chapter Seven

# Techniques to Fire up Your Life

In this part of the book learn how to fire up your finances, your career and your relationships with a series of special energy rituals. Each will boost your personal success, thereby enhancing your charisma and your inner strength.

Discover how a party can generate the chi that will help bind a family together, how symbols can draw in prosperity and how personal exercises can ensure that wishes are fulfilled. Improving your personal finances can be achieved in many ways: simply growing a plant in an auspicious area of the house or writing a dollar sign on your hand will be enough to cause a change.

Enjoy feeling your life improve as each tip will give an extra boost to your home life, bank balance and career.

# 144 Jump-starting a stagnant life

Placing a crystal geode in the northwest of your home brings you mentor luck, and the support of an influential mentor will create new opportunities in your life.

Use the eight aspirations formula of the Pa Kua to place feng shui symbols of good fortune in the different compass corners of the home. This is a simple yet effective formula in which each of the eight directions stands for a different desired goal.

### Stimulating relationships luck

If you want to fire up your relationships luck, bringing romance and love luck into your life, ensure that the southwest corner of your home is washed with bright lights to create fire energy. This, in turn, produces the earth element that brings nesting luck. Any symbol made of crystals – such as mandarin ducks and double happiness symbols of love – will jazz up your relationships luck tremendously.

### Activating career luck

If your life is stagnating due to lack of challenges, activate the north corner of your living room, or work area, with a water feature. A small aquarium will generate yang energy if you keep a few little fish that are active swimmers. This will make you upwardly mobile, bringing new opportunities and challenges into your work life. Energy from an aquarium is especially beneficial if you are developing a career in a big company.

### Generating recognition luck

Stagnation can also be caused by the constant disappointment of lack of success or not receiving positive feedback. If you want your work to be appreciated, and to gain recognition and praise, jump-start your creativity by bringing in the kind of chi that fosters encouragement and support into your life. Achieve this by placing lots of plants in the south. This stimulates the energy of the wood element, producing vital fire element energy. When you generate this kind of elemental flow in the south of your rooms, it activates your recognition luck, bringing you more attention.

### Attracting mentor luck

Finally, if you want to meet influential people who can open the right doors to new pathways in your life, jump-start your mentor luck. Nothing makes the adrenaline flow faster than having a worthwhile mentor 'adopt' you as a protégé, giving you the support and encouragement you need to achieve your goals. Attract this kind of luck by placing a large piece of crystal geode in the northwest of your home. The crystal geode exudes much-needed metal energy, bringing the mentor luck that will make all the difference to your life.

# Throw a party on a special day to reignite yang chi  145

One of the best ways to bring a blast of yang energy into your home is to throw an uplifting, noisy party. Invite a group of friends who care for you, whose auras glow with goodwill for you, and who are happy to come together in celebration of you. A birthday party is always excellent from this perspective.

When you are feeling down, nothing will cheer you more effectively than improving your home's energy with plenty of human chi. Ideally have live music but, if that is not possible, then playing any sort of happy music will be beneficial.

The hallmark of a good feng shui party is an abundance of food, goodwill and happiness energy. This will dissolve the negative energy that has got stuck in your home, transforming it into positive chi.

## Avoiding too much alcohol

However, your party should not become a big booze-up! Alcohol kills good energy so take care not to serve too much alcoholic drink. If you or your guests do get drunk, the goodwill energy of the party will evaporate, dissipating all the benefits of the earlier hours. An alcohol-drenched party is also likely to be followed by a hangover the next day, which depletes your chi further and brings your mood down. Always keep your party ambience happy, but not drunken.

Plentiful dishes of colourful food, served in a spirit of generosity, will get your party off to an excellent start – zinging with yang energy from the outset.

# 146   Hang a red Mandala on your south wall

One of feng shui's best-kept secrets is the power and efficacy of Mandalas, the symbols which signify the divine homes of the Buddhas. Mandalas can be circular, square, or a combination of the two. They reflect the powerful energies of heaven and earth which, when combined with the energy of the people living in the home, form the magnificent 'Power of Five' in Buddhist belief. This is the power of heaven, earth and humankind combined. In feng shui, this translates to the 'Power of Three'.

*Red is the colour of the south, so a red Mandala is best hung on a south wall. It will safeguard your home and bring good fortune from all directions.*

Mandalas usually have four doors that represent the four cardinal directions, attracting good luck from all sides. Having a Mandala in your home also ensures that the four doorways are properly safeguarded, protecting all the family.

### Good fortune from all directions

From the south the Mandala activates fire energy, which attracts a good name and the luck of fame and glory. From the north, water brings the luck of good food and plenty, success and prosperity. By stimulating the wood element in the east, the Mandala encourages good health and a long life. From the west, metal draws the luck of descendants to bring continuity and the happy sounds of children into the household.

### Paths to enlightenment

The four doorways also welcome the sacred Dharma, which opens pathways to eternal happiness and the highest wisdom. If you ever feel that life lacks meaning, or you are at a crossroads, hang a Mandala in your home. You will soon find that new pathways appear, providing the means to discover greater happiness.

# Place a water feature in the southwest  147

Wealth luck opens new possibilities and the power to liberate yourself from the bondage of a staid routine. In the years up to 2024, you can activate the powerful wealth-bringing potential of the 'Period of Eight'. Its indirect spirit resides in the southwest corner of the home, so placing a water feature here will be incredibly beneficial for your wealth luck. This is also an excellent way of keeping the feng shui of your home up-to-date for the current period.

### Digging a pond in the garden

To attract serious wealth into your life, the water feature you choose should be of substantial size – a pool or fishpond dug into the ground in the southwest of your garden, for example, is ideal. Make sure that the water is visible from inside your home, and keep it clean at all times.

Of course, whether you decide to activate the southwest area of your garden in this way will depend upon the space you have available to you. Although digging a pond is a major task, the rewards will be worthwhile and you will soon reap the benefits.

### Adding a water feature in a flat

If you live in a flat, a small water feature might be your only realistic option, so make the most of it. Choose a design, such as a six-tier waterfall, that showcases the movement of water. With clever use of lighting, you can keep the water glittering and sparkling as it flows. It is also important that the water is clean and keeps moving. This will create the yang energy needed to increase your wealth luck.

A bubbling fountain, or pond in which the water is constantly stirred by the movements of fish, will energize a southwest corner with yang chi, attracting wealth luck to your home.

# 148    Place a metal feature in the northwest

Protect the luck of the family's breadwinner by locating a metal feature in the north-west – the symbolic place of the father or leader – of your living room or bedroom. The metal object can be any one of the generic feng shui products, such as a metal windmill, a metallic fan or a Ksiddhigarbha's six rings staff. It could even be your stereo system or your computer. If your garage is in the north-west of your home, then your car counts as metal, making it auspicious here.

Metal energy serves as a strong protec-tion for your home, so including metal objects brings increased benefits. In 2008 and 2009 there is enormous lack of metal energy in the year's astrological chart, so having metal energy in the northwest will strengthen the luck of the house tremendously.

## Countering inauspicious room plans

If there is a toilet in the northwest of your home, strengthen the metal energy directly outside the room. If a store-room is located in the northwest of your home, it is best to open up the area into a living space and move your stored items elsewhere. Otherwise the patriarch's luck becomes locked up in the enclosed space. If the breadwinner in your family has experienced ill fortune, this will change when luck is released from a north-west store-room.

Most dangerous of all is a kitchen located in the northwest of your home. If you cannot relocate the kitchen, keep an urn of water in the room. Make sure that the urn is kept con-stantly full of water as this helps to counter harmful energy.

A Ksiddhigarbha's six rings staff is a traditional metal feng shui symbol, creating the powerful energy of the metal element in your home.

# Allowing yang energy into the facing palace 149 of your home

The facing palace is the part of the house where chi enters. It is always the space just inside the front door, often referred to as the hall or foyer. Keeping the main door opposite the facing palace open as much as possible allows a steady stream of revitalizing yang energy to enter the house.

Of course you need to consider security but, if you have a fence around your property, you might be able to keep the door into the house open – particularly if you have a dog that will bark at strangers. Feng shui celestial protectors, such as a pair of Fu dogs, will also guard the home from any harmful energy entering via the main door.

## Keeping halls clear of clutter

This facing palace must be kept clutter-free so that the energy remains auspicious at all times. Good energy here will flow into the rest of the house so long as it is not impeded. Never keep shoes or slippers here as this symbolizes the kicking out of the good chi coming in. Instead, keep your shoes inside a cupboard and hang the coats of visiting friends elsewhere, too.

Never allow old newspapers and magazines to pile up near the door to the facing palace. This kind of blockage will cause obstacles to manifest suddenly in your work and personal life. You might find, for example, that agreed-upon contracts suffer unexpected

A well-lit, spacious and clutter-free facing palace attracts beneficial chi into your home.

chi gathers in facing palace

chi flows from here into the home

setbacks and that previously sound relationships turn bad. A clutter-free, airy, brightly lit facing palace, however, allows chi to gather before entering your home, enhancing good fortune in all aspects of your life.

# 150 Place a painting of 100 birds just outside your front door

Pictures of birds bring good fortune – the more birds the better and it does not matter what type they are, although colourful plumage is particularly auspicious.

This wonderful tip has benefited so many people since I first suggested it that I am continuing to advise my readers to follow it. In feng shui, winged creatures symbolize a variety of opportunities that have the potential to change one's life for the better. Birds – especially birds with colourful plumage – not only bring good news into the home, but open your eyes to new creative ideas.

If you have ambitions to build and own a business, look for a painting of a hundred birds, a thousand birds, even a million birds – the more the better. If you can find a painting of a million birds – most will then be mere dots in the sky – and it appeals to you, invite it into your home as it is sure to bring you

good luck. In New York there is a famous art gallery that sells the work of a well-known Singaporean artist who paints nothing but millions of birds. His works sell in the millions and he has become rich just by selling his million-birds paintings.

## Birds are always auspicious
All kinds of birds can feature in your painting and bring you good luck. There is no such thing as a bird that brings bad news. Even crows – said to be messengers of the all-powerful, compassionate but wrathful gods – and owls, symbols of wisdom, have positive connotations despite some people believing that they bring bad luck.

# Create a lucky mountain star in your living room 151

Fire up the relationships in your life with the lucky mountain star. In flying star feng shui the auspicious mountain star not only brings good health and a long life, but amazing relationship luck. With the help of the lucky mountain star, you will be very popular, surrounded by friends and invited to every party.

## Short cut to good luck

You do not have to understand flying star feng shu to create an auspicious mountain star in your living room using this great short cut.

Firstly, place a waist-level table or sideboard in the corner of the room diagonally opposite the main front door. On top of this, place a crystal geode – the larger the geode and the more it resembles a mountain the better. It is even more auspicious if you can find a crystal geode mountain with three peaks. If you prefer, you can use an amethyst geode but only if it forms a mountain shape rather than a hole.

Next, shine a bright light on your crystal geode to activate it, bringing its benefits to life and helping it to exude the energy that attracts excellent relationships and friendship luck. When you create a lucky mountain in your living room it also activates the 'Period of Eight' luck, as the element of eight is earth.

*When looking for a suitable crystal or amethyst geode, keep in mind the shape of mountain peaks.*

# Fire up your finances with a six-level waterfall 152

This specially designed water feature can be placed indoors to activate the water star eight of the flying star charts, as well as the indirect spirit of the southwest. If you do not know where the water star eight of your home is located, place the waterfall in the southwest, north, east or southeast corner of your living room – all of these corners benefit from the presence of water.

In feng shui the number six stands for 'heaven energy', so the six levels of the waterfall symbolize water coming from heaven. A three-peaked mountain behind the waterfall attracts success to the next generation, and so is especially beneficial for families with children. The three peaks are as beneficial as the 'dragon gate' at the source of the 'river', which transforms carps into dragons.

The waterfall is lit by a five-colour light, which signifies the five elements and enhances the corner where the feature is placed with more energizing chi. Make sure the water keeps flowing.

*Flowing water brings yang energy and wealth luck to your home.*

# 153   Wear the transformational fan pendant in gold

The fan is a powerful symbol that can transform bad luck into good. In China, the importance of the fan is legendary. Imperial courtiers were rarely without their fans, which were reputed to ward off the bad vibes of negative gossip. Through history, fans were used as a symbolic protection against the ill intentions of jealous colleagues and associates. In modern times the fan continues to be used to bring about a change in fortune in homes suffering from excessive bad luck.

## Transforming your luck

If you or your family has undergone a series of mishaps, or a bout of illness, wearing a fan pendant will bring good luck back into your life. A gold fan pendant is best because you need the metal energy of gold. Wear the fan day and night, and keep it on for at least three months. Your luck will improve within the first couple of weeks. Once your bad luck is totally transformed to good luck you need not continue wearing the pendant. However, keep it safe because you never know when you might need it again.

The fan is a potent symbol in Chinese tradition and feng shui, not only protecting its owner against the effects of harmful energy but actively transforming bad luck into good fortune.

# Wear the wish-fulfilling mantra ring 154
## at all times

Sacred mantras, which originated in ancient Sanskrit, are believed to have been transmitted directly from the Buddha. They are sacred sounds that symbolize the divine power of the highest consciousness within us. The empowerments they invoke are limitless in their benefits, although how they manifest themselves depends on the mind of the individual reciting them. All sacred mantras have great power but different mantras bring different benefits.

Buddhists believe that chanting, writing and wearing mantras can protect individuals and help them to develop progressively higher levels of consciousness.

### Achieving your goals

The wish-fulfilling mantra – also known as the 'Mantra of the Lotus Pinnacle of Buddha Amoghapasha' – helps you achieve your desires when worn or chanted. Your goals can be for spiritual, emotional, mental, physical and material fulfilment.

You can wear the mantra:

OM PADMO USHNISHA
VIMALE HUM PHAT

Whether inscribed on a ring or printed in Chinese calligraphy on fabric, sacred mantras have great power. They not only help us to achieve our desires but also to find inner peace.

on the inner face of a mantra ring and enhance the benefits it brings to your love life, your relationships, family, health, career success or prosperity by also reciting it.

Wear the mantra ring on any finger or as a pendant around your neck. Keeping this ring on your body will create a protective aura and defend against negative vibes. It also plants the seeds of the blessings that come from constantly being near holy words. The effect is to create within you a sense of calmness and a feeling of great compassion towards fellow human beings.

# 155 Write the dollar sign on your hand every day for 15 day

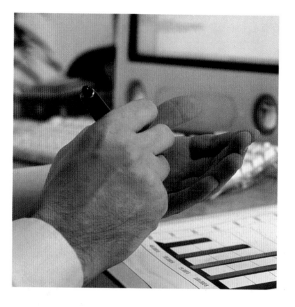

To increase your prosperity write your chosen currency sign in red ink on the palm of your hand on the day of the New Moon and for the 15 days of the waxing Moon.

This is a contemporary interpretation of an old Taoist ritual, which used to be extremely popular amongst students of the Tao. I first came across this ritual as a youngster when I was taught to write the word Fook, or 'Luck', on my palm.

I forgot all about the ritual until I lived in Hong Kong during my corporate and businesswoman days. At this time, an old Taoist practitioner told me to write the dollar sign on the palm of my right hand on a New Moon day. After that I was to keep writing the dollar sign on my palm for all 15 days of the waxing moon. Guess what – I soon succeeded in packaging a deal to buy control of a department store. That deal was eventually a success and since then I have recommended this ritual privately with equal success.

## Use red cinnabar for the strongest effect

Use red cinnabar to write your dollar sign. If you have a different currency sign for your country – such as the pound, yen or yuan – by all means use it instead of the dollar sign. There is often something magical about the signs that indicate currency, just as there is an empowering quality to red ink – especially cinnabar. As you write, concentrate your thoughts so that the sign is imbued with the power of your belief and positive energy.

# Wear mantra gold jewellery to attract 156 beneficial chi

There are many beautiful mantras that can be worn as gold jewellery. Fashioning a mantra in gold is a wonderful way to invoke the power of these holy syllables and sounds, activating a special, divine energy.

The wearing of sacred mantras as adornments is not so much feng shui as inspired by feng shui. I discovered that the traditions of Tibetan Buddhism include many rituals that appear similar to those of feng shui except that Buddhism uses many spiritual syllables and symbols to attract good fortune or to protect against misfortune.

I have been studying and researching Tibetan Buddhist rituals now for ten years, and have discovered many wonderful symbols, mantras and rituals of protection and luck enhancement. Wearing mantra gold jewellery is one of the most popular ways to safeguard against misfortune, spirit harm and other kinds of bad luck.

## Popular mantras

Of the many mantras fashioned into pendants, bracelets and rings perhaps the most widely worn continue to be those that carry the most popular mantras, that of Tara, Mother of all the Buddhas:

OM TARE TUTTARE TURE SOHA

meaning 'may the meaning of the mantra take hold in my mind' and the mantra of the Compassionate Buddha:

OM MANI PADME HUMA

All the teachings of the Buddha are contained in this mantra, which cannot be translated into a simple phrase. It invokes benevolence and empathy for all living things.

In addition you can also look for powerful seed syllables such as OM or HUM that are made from gold and fashioned into pendants. These pendants may take on the guise of personal adornment but they are really centres of powerful protective energy. When you wear them, visualize rays of blessing light emanating from them. This kind of visualization activates their power tremendously. If you feel in any kind of danger, or have any sort of premonition, rub the pendant and recite the mantra. You will find that your fears subside instantly, leaving you feeling a lot calmer.

Wearing gold mantra jewellery and visualizing its powerful positive energy is a wonderful way to enhance your spirituality and ward off bad luck.

# 157 Energizing a room with the Sun and Moon sign

The signs of the Sun and the Moon have an empowering energy, particularly when combined. The New Moon is perceived as a crescent shape and the Sun is visualized as a full circle. Together they form the Sun and Moon sign which, over time, has evolved into the Chinese gold ingot. The New Moon forms the base, with its ends tilted upwards, and the Sun appears above it.

## Yin and yang balance

The Sun and Moon sign has several auspicious connotations. Firstly, it signifies the balance of yin and yang, with the Moon being yin and the Sun being yang. The sign also represents night and day when moonlight and sunlight wash the Earth with light.

Moonlight brings serenity, enabling people to rebuild their strength and stamina even as they rest, while sunlight brings life, harvest and prosperity. One cannot exist without the other. If you have no time to rest the body and rejuvenate, your mind and spirit will not be able to make the most of the Sun's light and energy. Together the Sun and the Moon are a powerful energizing force.

An auspiciously placed mirror in the shape of the Sun will reflect yang energy into your home.

The shapes of Chinese gold ingots are based on the Sun and Moon signs.

## Activating the power of the signs

As Chinese ingots not only signify the Sun and the Moon but are a symbol of wealth and prosperity, they are a wonderful symbol of good luck in your home.

Another way to bring the illuminating energy of the Sun and the Moon into your home is to hang a drawing or an embroidery of the signs in your living room. Reflect on the power of the signs to activate their energy.

# Paint your southeast deep blue to jump start wealth luck 158

According to the Pa Kua formula of feng shui the southeast location of the home is the wealth corner. The element of the southeast corner is wood – symbolic of growth – which is activated by water. By energizing the southeast corner with the wood and water elements, you will immediately create fast-growing wealth luck.

While the presence of water in the southeast corner is very auspicious, it may not be practical. When a room is too small for a water feature, you can paint one wall in a shade of blue that creates a similar energy effect to water and increases your prosperity.

## Deep blue suggests water

Locate the southeast wall of your favourite room. This might be your bedroom or a room where the family spends a lot of time such as the living room. Paint the southeast wall a deep blue suggestive of deep water. This feature wall, signifying the presence of water, emanates wood energy that produces growth chi. Your whole family will benefit. You may also want to implement the same concept in your office, where a deep blue wall in the southeast will increase profits.

## Avoiding excessive yin

Paint only the southeast wall. Resist the urge to get carried away and paint the whole room – it would instantly become excessively yin, symbolically drowning the residents. This is true even in rooms such as the bedroom and bathroom, where it is acceptable to have more yin than in other living areas.

Siting wood furniture against a blue southeast wall allows the wood element to activate the water element, enhancing your wealth luck.

### ENERGY TIP

## Locating the southeast wall

Use a compass to locate the southeast wall. Standing in the centre of the room, first establish the north wall then note the orientation of the other walls.

Remember, you can choose your favourite rooms at home and paint the southeast wall blue, but also apply this to your office at work – a blue southeast wall here will help increase your company's profits.

# 159 Place sea salt or rock salt inside your wallet to attract cash luck

Sea salt, or natural rock salt, created by the oceans of the world, is one of the most powerful tools used in feng shui. Its strong energy not only gives it great cleansing properties but the capacity to attract wealth. While it is well known that natural salt is an effective cleanser of bad chi – explaining why it is so effective for purifying old furniture and revitalizing antique objects (see Tip 31) – its attraction properties are less well known.

*Natural sea salt has powerful attractive properties.*

According to the Taoists, sewing several grains of sea salt into a small pouch in your wallet will attract cash into it.

A useful tip for anyone who enjoys playing the tables at a casino, or sitting down to a friendly game of poker, is to carry a wallet filled to overflowing with cash and place some sea salt with it. This ensures money does not leave your wallet. Note that sea salt melts and dissolves over time so you will need to refill your pouch or wallet on a regular basis.

# 160 Sprout a plant in the southeast to bring in a new source of income

The Chinese are extremely fond of sprouting new plants. Not only do new plants signify the energy of springtime and a successful beginning, but they serve as an omen of good fortune. The southeast corner of your home is the wealth corner and the place of wood energy. By placing sprouting plants here, you simulate the auspicious presence of sheng chi. According to Eight Mansions feng shui, sheng chi is the most important type of chi. Sheng chi is growth chi, and it imparts an expanding yang energy vital to overall feng shui luck.

**Imparting wealth energy to your home**
Feng shui is particularly beneficial to anyone wanting to create multiple sources of income. While there are several feng shui practices for creating wealth energy in the home, the constant presence of plants growing strongly in the southeast is one of the most effective. If there is no growth here, wealth energy becomes increasingly depleted.

Each new plant that sprouts and grows successfully in a southeast corner will create a new source of income for you or a member of your family.

# Place a red jewel in earth corners for 161 wealth luck

Wish-fulfilling jewels bring good luck when placed in earth corners in the southwest, northeast and centre of your home. Display them prominently on tables or sideboards, shining light at them for best effect.

## Overcoming obstacles to prosperity

To dissolve hostile energy, select a red wish-fulfilling jewel. Wrap it in a red or yellow cloth and bury it in the southwest or northeast of your garden. Alternatively, if you live in a flat without a garden, place the red jewel on a glass saucer in a southwest or northeast corner. If you are sensing obstacles to your prosperity luck, this ritual will help you to overcome them.

You can also use wish-fulfilling jewels to enhance earth energy in whichever corner of your home is most auspicious for the coming year. In 2008 the east corner is luckiest and a blue jewel will enhance its energy. In 2009 the southeast corner, also best activated by a blue jewel, is most auspicious. In 2010, the best place to have wish-fulfilling jewels is in the centre of the house. Earth chi is grounding and enhances financial stability in your home, so it is well worth you carrying out these simple rituals.

Wish-fulfilling jewels, made of crystal or glass, are an easy way to enhance good luck.

# Display a monkey on a horse to get a 162 promotion

Displaying the auspicious symbol of a monkey on a horse is one of the easiest and most effective ways of jump-starting your career luck. If you have been waiting for a promotion that has not materialized, invest in the monkey riding a horse symbol. This is particularly effective in enhancing the upward mobility of a young career person. Place the symbol in either the location of the horse (the south) or in the location of the monkey (the southwest). Let the image face the door if possible.

## Other auspicious animal symbols

If you are a senior manager hoping for promotion to the top job, select a monkey sitting on an elephant instead to symbolize high office. Elephants have many auspicious meanings, which is why they are revered in many Asian cultures. Displaying a monkey on an elephant

suggests you will become a leader with many supporters. The symbol is therefore particularly suitable for politicians.

## Using the four friends

The Buddhist symbolism of the four friends is particularly auspicious. It features a rabbit and bird sitting on top of the monkey riding the horse. The bird flies, the rabbit runs, the monkey swings through the trees and the elephant uses its strength and size to assist you. In this way you are symbolically helped to achieve your goals.

Metal energy works faster and more efficiently, so look for the symbol in brass.

# 163 Create an aquarium filled with little fish for career luck

It is possible to benefit from the positive chi of swimming fish no matter the size of your room. The curving sides of a large aquarium and small goldfish bowl denote a smooth, constant path to wellbeing and prosperity.

To boost your career luck, activate a north corner in your home. Locate the north corner of a room where you spend much of your time then place an aquarium here. The strong swimming action of small fish provides a constant source of yang energy. If you have a large enough aquarium, you can further enhance good chi by having fish in multiples of nine.

## Keeping healthy fish is good chi

Aquariums are excellent as feng shui activators so long as they are properly maintained. Keep the aquarium well aerated so that the water does not become stagnant and the fish have a plentiful supply of oxygen. If the fish start dying, the water quality is probably not good enough. However, if one or two die for no apparent reason it is possible that they have absorbed your bad luck.

# Firing up your love life with plum blossom luck 164

Creating plum blossom luck is an effective way to bring in marriage opportunities. Placing one or more of the traditional symbols of love – a pair of birds, the double happiness sign, the dragon and the phoenix – in the southwest corner of your home is all you need to do to activate plum blossom luck.

## Finding a suitable mate
Plum blossom luck can work for or against you, however. At best, the person you attract will be someone good natured and dependable who will make you happy throughout your life. You need to beware, though, of attracting the opposite – a person who is not suitable for you, and who will cause you heartache and problems. It is not enough to create the energy of marriage, you need to take steps to attract a good mate. For this, you must add peach blossom luck.

## Activating peach blossom luck
For peach blossom luck, first identify your personal peach blossom animal. This will be either the Horse, the Rooster, the Rabbit or the Rat. In feng shui, only these four animals of the cardinal signs are counted as peach blossom animals. Place a symbol of your peach blossom animal in a prominent place in its corresponding part of your home – the Rat is located in the north, the Horse in the south, the Rabbit in the east and the Rooster in the west.

Secondly, identify the peach blossom location for this year or the coming one. In 2008 it is in the northeast, in the south in 2009 and in the north in 2010. Activate the sector with a symbol of your peach blossom animal. Unless yours is the Rooster, this will necessitate finding more than one peach blossom animal symbol for both auspicious locations in your home.

*Plum blossom luck energizes your love life with new possibilities. Beware, though, that the potential mates it attracts may be good or bad for you.*

### ENERGY TIP
## Your peach blossom animal
Your peach blossom animal is governed by your Chinese Zodiac sign. If you were born in the year of the Rooster, the Snake or the Ox, your peach blossom animal is the Horse; for the Dragon, the Rat or the Monkey, it is the Rooster; for the Rabbit, the Sheep or the Boar, it is the Rat; and for the Tiger, the Horse or the Dog, it is the Rabbit.

# 165   Golden Roosters in the west bring love and strength

The Golden Rooster is the peach blossom animal of those born in the years of the Dragon, the Rat and the Monkey. People born under these signs are action-oriented – the great competitors of the Chinese Zodiac. Such positive and determined individuals are unlikely to need much help in the love and marriage aspects of their lives. The Dragon is confident and head-strong, the Rat is opportunistic and ambitious while the Monkey is clever and creative. However, if love has eluded you despite your promising Chinese Zodiac sign, it's now time to turn to the Dragon's secret ally – the Rooster or Cockerel.

## Selecting a lucky Rooster

Search for a Rooster symbol with a distinguished appearance that best represents the type of person you are looking for. If you want a good-natured, successful mate, it makes sense to choose a Rooster symbol that emanates positive vibes.

There are many versions of the proud Rooster but the best of all is the golden Rooster. You can also find embroidered versions surrounded by jewels, looking very rich indeed. Make sure you acquire the Rooster that is to be your peach blossom animal from a shop that looks clean and well fitted out. Do not buy from roadside stalls or from someone who annoys you. The Rooster that you choose to introduce into your environment should have been surrounded by good energy at all times.

When you bring the Rooster indoors, immediately place it on a high shelf or table in the west corner of your home.

To find your ideal mate, choose a golden Rooster that emanates positive energy.

# 166   Bejewelled Rats in the north draw love and wealth luck

A bejewelled Rat with a happy expression is sure to bring success in your love life.

The Rat brings wealth and continued prosperity, and is the peach blossom animal of those born under the signs of the Rabbit, the Sheep and the Boar. This trio of signs are the diplomats of the Chinese Zodiac. Sensible people, they are sensitive to the feelings of others, caring and eager to please. If you were born under the Rabbit, the Sheep or the Boar signs, and want to settle down with a good partner, activate your love luck by placing an image of the Rat in the north of your home. For the best results, look for a bejewelled Rat and purchase it from a shop that gives you good vibes.

## Bejewelled Rabbits in the east attract 167 romance and marriage

The Rabbit is the peach blossom animal of those born in the years of the Tiger, the Horse and the Dog. As the Rabbit is the secret friend of the Dog this peach blossom animal works the most powerfully for those born in the year of the Dog.

People born in the trinity of Tiger, Horse and Dog possess an independence of spirit that sets them apart form others in the Chinese Zodiac. They are not easy to pin down in marriage and may then suddenly realize that marriage opportunities may have passed them by. Emotional and highly principled people, they are also impetuous and restless. The Tiger growls and is impatient, the Horse runs at a fast and furious gallop, while the good-natured Dog is the most calming presence within the trinity. Their peach blossom animal is the Rabbit whose first instinct is to run as fast as possible.

### Finding a beautiful rabbit

Search for a bejewelled Rabbit – one that is sitting on a bed of coins will attract extra good fortune. Acquire this symbol from a really nice sales person in a welcoming, attractive shop. Let the rabbit come to you under pleasing circumstances, then place it high in the east corner of your bedroom.

A white bejewelled rabbit is very auspicious.

## Crystal Horses in the south inspire 168 affection and recognition

The Horse is the peach blossom animal of those born in the years of the Rooster, the Snake and the Ox. This is the trinity of intellectuals in the Chinese Zodiac; to these signs belong the thinkers and visionaries who are also pragmatists. All three signs are known for their poise and confidence, have a resoluteness of character and possess formidable capabilities that make them especially choosy when it comes to settling down with a mate. Their peach blossom animal is the independent, restless and free-spirited Horse.

### Looking for a noble Horse

Search for a crystal or crystal-studded Horse, or Horses, and place the symbol prominently in a south corner. By using this method to attract a mate, you will find someone who brings you the joy of both affection and recognition. The Horse is a noble creature whose presence in the home always brings victory and success.

The Victory Horse (left) helps you outperform the competition. The Tribute Horse, which is loaded with jewels, brings prosperity. The Wind-horse protects from physical harm.

# Index

# Picture Credits

## Photography

Simon Barber 20 (bottom).
CICO: Geoff Dann 37 (bottom);
Jacqui Mair 117.
Elizabeth Whiting & Associates 22.
Elizabeth Whiting & Associates: Tommy
Candler 14 (top); Yvonne Carylon 27
(top right); Michael Dunne 30; Rodney
Hyett 19, 33 (top middle); Tom
Leighton 66 (bottom); Neil Lorimer 52;
Mark Luscombe-Whyte 154 (top);
Friedhelm Thomas 27 (bottom).
Getty Images: altrendo images 17 (top);
Peter Anderson 33 (top right); Eric
Audras 111 (top); Karen Beard 106
(bottom); Annabelle Breakey 137, 154
(bottom); Asia Images 89, 95 (left);
BLOOMimage 133 (bottom); Gareth
Brown 13; Gary Burchell 114 (top left);
Lauren Burke 135 (top); C Squared
Studio 75; Angelo Cavalli 57 (bottom),
112, 130 (top); Chabruken 113; Gary
Chowanetz 47; Frederic Cirou 110; DAJ
114 (bottom); Digital Vision 132 (top);
DKAR Images 57 (top); Thierry Dosogne
148 (top); John Dowland 109; Harrison
Eastwood 148 (bottom); Dorling
Kindersley 153 (top); Wayne Eastep 40;
Neil Emmerson 1, 90, 128 (top); Pieter
Estersohn 77; Don Farrall 80; Safia
Fatimi 92 (left); Malcolm Fife 63
(bottom); Jules Frazier 23 (top); Gallo
Images/Emielke van Wyk 108 (top);
Gazimal 152 (bottom); Glowimages 25;
Gone Wild Limited 126; Michelangelo
Gratton 145 (top); Paul Grebliunas 104
(top); Stuart Gregory 76 (bottom); Peter
Gridley 146; Tom Grill 99 (bottom); ML
Harris 64 (bottom); Brian Harrison 107
(top); K; Hatt 39 (bottom); Ken Hayden
51; Huntley Headworth 92, 151; Noel
Hendrickson 35 (bottom); Meredith
Hever 58 (top); Ando & Utagawa
Hiroshige 127 (bottom right); Walter
Hodges 69 (top); Stephan Hoeck 8, 73;
Steven Hunt 120; Ivan Hunter 143;
Image Source 17 (bottom), 28 (top), 86
(bottom), 152 (top); Imagemore 55, 83
(bottom), 118 (top); Images Inc/Alex
Cao 92 (right); Sian Irvine 65; Erik
Isakson 132 (bottom); Isu 141 (top);
Ilisa Katz 35 (top); Barnabus Kindersley
38, 43 (top right); Yuka Kisugi 48 (top);
Darrin Klimek 88; Lars Klove 44; Junichi
Kusaka 29; Justin Lightley 135 (bottom);
Mark Lund 97 (top); Alex Mares-Manton
147 (bottom); Simon McBride 59; Ryan
McVay 133 (top), 134 (top); Rob
Melnychuk 31, 34 (top); Dana Menussi
45; Microzoa 43 (bottom), 103; Robert
Mizono 128 (bottom); Daisuke Morito
155 (top); Laurence Mouton 96; Bryan
Mullennix 23 (bottom); Philip Nealey 60
(top); Neo Vision 78 (top); Thomas
Northcut 67 (top), 111 (bottom), 130
(bottom); Rosanne Olson 63 (top); Max
Oppenheim 114 (top right); Don
Paulson 42 (bottom left); Victoria
Pearson 141 (bottom); Kevin Phillips
102; Javier Pierini 9; Andrea Pistolesi
91; Justin Pomfrey 100; Martin Poole 81
(right), 107 (bottom); Spike Powell 37
(top); Pat Powers & Cherryl Schafer 74
(bottom); Siede Pries 23 (bottom right);
Stephanie Rauser 139; Red Cover 48
(bottom), 70, 108 (bottom); Trinette
Reed 34 (bottom), 85, 95 (right); Ed
Reeve 42 (bottom middle); John A Rizzo
64 (top); rubberball 81 (left); Koichi
Saito 79 (top); Jeremy Samuelson 53
(top); Tatsuhiko Sawada 83 (top); Gregor
Schuster 138; Jon Shireman 20 (top);
Ariel Skelley 101; Simon Songhurst 98;
Phillip & Karen Spears 16; Phillip Spears
15; Siri Stafford 42 (top); Kim Steele 61;
Stockbyte 11, 14 (bottom), 28 (bottom),
66 (top), 69 (bottom), 84, 106 (top),
122; Stockdisc 134 (bottom); Studio
Paggy 79 (bottom); Keren Su 56; Meg
Takamura 10, 118 (bottom); Maria
Teijeiro 105; Alan Thornton 43 (top
left); Debi Treloar 24; Kris Timken 86
(top); Caroline von Tuempling 115;
Michael Turek 27 (top left); Amanda
Turner 54; UHB Trust 76 (top); Nick
Veasey 4 (top), 116; Steven Weinberg 2,
129 (top); Adrian Weinbrecht 39 (top);
James Worrell 99 (top); Jun Yamashita
131 (top); ZenShui/Alix Minde 87; Max
Zerrahn 21; Norma Zuniga 74 (top).
Lillian Too/WOFS.com 4 (bottom), 5, 6
(both), 7, 23 (middle), 82, 121, 123,
124, 125, 127 (top), 131 (bottom),
136, 138 (top right), 140, 142, 144,
145 (bottom), 147 (top), 149, 150
(bottom), 153 (bottom), 155 (bottom),
156 (both), 157 (both).
Loupe: 36 (bottom), 49, 62, 68, 150
(top); David Montgomery 3, 50; Chris
Everard 46; Henry Bourne 53 (bottom),
67 (bottom); Christopher Drake 58
(bottom); Geoff Dann 63 (bottom right);
Polly Wreford 71; David Brittain 78
(bottom), 129 (bottom); Claire
Richardson 97 (bottom); Melanie Eclare
104 (bottom).Superstock 36 (top).
Warren Photographic: Jane Burton 60
(bottom).

## Illustration

Kate Simunek/CICO 52.
Stephen Dew/CICO 13, 15, 18, 19, 20,
21, 22, 26 (both), 29, 30, 32, 33, 40,
41, 44, 46, 47, 51, 54, 56, 61, 62, 65,
77, 90, 91, 93, 119, 120, 121, 123
(both), 124, 125, 126, 143.
Anthony Duke/CICO 16, 24, 35, 45, 68,
72, 82, 94, 100, 101, 102.